CASTLES &
STRONGHOLDS

CASTLES & STRONGHOLDS

RICHARD MUIR

MACMILLAN
LONDON

First published in the United Kingdom 1990 by
MACMILLAN LONDON LIMITED
4 Little Essex Street London WC2R 3LF
and Basingstoke

Associated companies in Auckland, Delhi, Dublin, Gaborone,
Hamburg, Harare, Hong Kong, Johannesburg, Kuala Lumpur,
Lagos, Manzini, Melbourne, Mexico City, Nairobi, New York,
Singapore and Tokyo

A CIP catalogue record for this book is available from the British
Library.

ISBN 0–333–47119–9

Designed by Behram Kapadia
Typeset by Rowland Phototypesetting Limited
Bury St Edmunds, Suffolk
Printed in Spain

Contents

INTRODUCTION

Castles are generally associated with the age of chivalry, with bold gestures, bright armour and waving banners. In reality, however, they are monuments to the dark sides of human nature, to fear, distrust and insecurity. Conflict and the building of defenceworks to resist attackers seem to have existed for as long as people have been sufficiently numerous to compete for the control of territory. Recent discoveries have shown that even in the distant New Stone Age, once perceived as a golden age of innocent pioneering, warfare became endemic and great strongholds were built.

Strongholds were not built for comfort or convenience. Usually they consumed a great deal of hard toil, willingly or reluctantly given, and were built to meet a particular threat. However, they mirrored not only the current methods of warfare but also the prevailing social values. The greater of the prehistoric fortresses were primarily communal strongholds but they also seem to have had significant economic and ritual uses. The fortresses, town and coastal defences built by the Romans represented a different kind of attempt to preserve the status quo; they were colonial strongholds quite comparable to those built in colonial territories by the European powers in the nineteenth century. With the passing of Roman power in Britain there was a return to the building of communal strongholds, the *burhs*, which were usually garrisoned towns. These could resist Danish attack and generate commercial activities to strengthen the bond between the community and its setting.

The castles which the Normans introduced were different again. Initially built to pacify the newly conquered territories, they became the private strongholds of particular families and dynasties. They provided protection for the nobles who built them and they also controlled the surrounding territory. No attack could succeed so long as the lord and his retainers remained secure within the castle and free to sally forth as soon as the siege was lifted. The medieval castle was also very much a product of the feudal system, and when that system was eroded, so its role came into question. On the Continent many castles endured far beyond the Middle Ages but in England and Wales the emergence of a strong central power in the form of the Tudor dynasty meant the demise of the private fortress.

At the same time a new sense of national identity began to emerge and the carefully considered artillery forts constructed by Henry VIII were not created to resist an internal challenge but to protect the nation against invasion and subjugation by a foreign power. For some centuries afterwards, the maintenance of a strong fleet and a hard outer shell of defences constituted a credible and effective system of national defence. But today, aircraft and missiles can by-pass any such system of frontier defences and strike directly at the soft interior of the national territory. Centuries of evolution have failed to produce an impregnable stronghold while the development of military architecture has simply encouraged parallel development in offensive warfare.

I have not attempted to write a comprehensive guidebook to the castles and strongholds of Britain. To be in any meaningful sense comprehensive, such a book would be far too large to sit within its covers. Rather, I have sought to provide a text which will assist the reader to understand the lay-out and former life of any castle visited. While paying due attention to the evolution of military architecture, I have also included chapters which explore other aspects of the stronghold. I have described not only the castle at war but also the castle at peace, and have highlighted both the building and the destruction of castles. In these ways I have tried to bring the subject to life and portray castles and strongholds as living places – not simply assemblages of earth, stone and mortar.

Chapter One

The ramparts of Maiden
Castle.

THE ANCIENT STRONGHOLDS

S trongholds are, by and large, expressions of the insecurity of the people who build them. Occasionally they might be created to advertise the status and the might of those who commanded their construction but even so, without conflict – or the threat of conflict – there would be no hillforts, castles or redoubts. Some will argue that the urge to fight and kill our fellows is an inherent part of human nature, others that war is an unnatural state induced by flaws in society. The ancient fossil evidence of human evolution in Africa can be, and has been, interpreted in different ways. These interpretations tend to tell one more about the political outlook of the authors than about the instincts and drives inherited from our distant ancestors. Whatever the truth, the prehistoric strongholds of Britain are numerous, varied and sometimes still imposing. Most of them reflect the pressing need to protect the community which held the surrounding territory against outsiders who would have liked to hold it – and who might resort to war to realise their ambition. Had life-giving land not been in short supply there would have been little reason to fight over it.

When the glaciers and ice sheets of the last Ice Age withdrew into the mountain fastnesses some ten or twelve thousand years ago, Britain was recolonised both by people and by woodland. Ways of life were established which centred on the hunting of wild animals and the gathering of shellfish and of vegetable resources such as edible nuts, fruits, roots and shoots. Small groups, probably clan-like federations of extended families, followed migratory existences in order to exploit the different natural resources as they became available. Some groups might spend the winter at a lake shore site in lowland woodlands and disperse into upland hunting grounds in summer, and others migrate between the sea shore and inland hunting ranges. In such ways clan territories will have formed which enclosed the array of seasonal resources needed to sustain each community.

As the numbers of these Middle Stone Age people increased, so each group will have encountered its neighbours and territorial boundaries will have had to be negotiated. No evidence of warfare or of strongholds dating from these times is known, but it would be surprising if skirmishes and diplomacy had not existed. Any group robbed of access to resources which it needed in one season of the year faced a grim future. The problem with understanding the role of conflict in most prehistoric societies is that weapons used in hunting and tools such as axes, mattocks or hammers could just as easily have served as arms for killing people.

Around 7000 years ago farming was introduced to Britain. As the dependence on crops increased, so the bond between a family and their land was tightened. Much is still to be learned about the pioneer farmers. There could easily have been a fundamental conflict between those who cleared, tilled and enclosed the land and sought to exclude or eliminate wild animals and others who still depended on deer and wild ponies and cattle for their livelihood. But eventually, groups merged to form larger clans or tribes, and settlements which operated as local capitals or trading centres emerged. During the post-Second-World-War period a number of these 'central places' of the New Stone Age have been discovered, along with the evidence of the wars, raids or skirmishes which destroyed them.

Crickley Hill lies on the edge of the Cotswolds about four miles (6.4km) south of Cheltenham and commands fine views across the valley of the Severn. Archaeological excavations began here in 1969 and are still continuing. Initially the work involved a small-scale exploration of what seemed to be an unexceptional Iron Age hillfort. However, interest in the site was heightened when traces of 'Neolithic' or New Stone Age relics were discovered lying near the centre of the much later hillfort, signs of the first Neolithic habitations to be unearthed in the Cotswolds. During the Neolithic period (about 5000–2500 BC) a number of large 'causewayed enclosures' were built in different parts of England, often on hilltop sites. Roughly circular or oval in plan, the interior, which might have served as a regional centre for trading and for ritual, was surrounded by one or more rings of interrupted banks and ditches. The fact that these once imposing earthworks were broken by causeways seemed to argue against the enclosure being built for defence and they are sometimes regarded as the prehistoric equivalents of the great medieval fair sites.

The Crickley Hill enclosure was tiny in comparison to most others, only two acres (0.8ha) in area, and consisted at first of two circuits of ditches breached by numerous entrance causeways. The Neolithic discoveries on the site fall between the dates c. 3000–2600 BC. The enclosure was abandoned and rebuilt on at least two occasions and then, after another period of abandonment, it was reconstructed with a single encircling ditch with just a few narrow entrances and a strong palisade and fences. Inside the enclosure a small plateau had been separated from the rest of the interior by an intricate system of fences and could be reached by a footpath guarded by two gates. The footpath led to a platform with low mounds of stone containing bones, pottery and flint at its extremities. A small rectangular building, interpreted as a shrine, stood beside a little courtyard, with a hearth lying just in front of the building. Later the footpath was systematically buried under a great cairn of rubble and a circle of stones was built upon the remains of the building, surrounding a great stone slab on which materials were burned. A trench was cut to isolate this peculiar sacred area from its surroundings.

Thus far one might seem to be encountering a sequence of small and rather mysterious causewayed enclosures which eventually developed to enclose a shrine used for some unfathomable form of worship and which continued to attract devotees until the beginning of the Bronze Age. The excavations, however, revealed clear evidence of defenceworks and of one of the first battles known to have been fought on British soil. The earliest enclosure had at least nineteen causeways across the surrounding ditch system but only five of these gaps also breached the encircling bank as well. Each gap was closed by a gate with massive gateposts while fences flanked the road to the inner gate, continuing into the interior where the traces of habitations were found. Each of the successive enclosures produced finds of leaf-shaped flint arrowheads and each was, amongst other things, a defended settlement. The last of the successive enclosures must have fallen after a particularly determined attack – almost 400 of the arrows fired in this assault have been recovered and their positions show that they were aimed at defenders massed around two entrances and the palisade of the bank between them. (Some of the arrows had overshot their mark and landed inside the defences.) When the attack was successful, the gates were stormed and the dwellings inside the fortifications were burned.

The Crickley Hill site had an obvious defensive value and much later it was fortified by two successive Iron Age hillforts. At the close of the Roman period two separate settlements, one housing peasants and the other the defended base of a noble, were built about 655 feet (200m) apart within the ruined Iron Age ramparts. The hillfort and the Dark Age settlements perished violently, as the Neolithic settlement had done long before, in flames.

While archaeological work at Crickley Hill was proceeding, other defended Neolithic settlements were recognised. Hambledon Hill in Dorset is one of the most impressive of Britain's Iron Age hillforts. Just outside the Iron Age fortification is a much older Neolithic causewayed enclosure of eighteen acres (7.2ha) which, when excavated in 1974–7, was found to have many skulls spaced out at intervals in its ditch. Closer inspection of the hill has revealed another causewayed enclosure and this Neolithic assemblage of monuments was guarded by massive outworks which cut off the approaches to the hill and enclosed no less than 100 acres (40ha) of ground.

About one-fifth of the ditches surrounding the main enclosure were excavated and, in addition to the thirty skulls which punctuated the floor of the first ditch, skeletal remains representing at least seventy individuals were found. The excavator, Dr Roger Mercer, was tempted to suggest that 'the main enclosure at Hambledon was a vast reeking open cemetery, its silence broken only by the din of crows and ravens'. He thought the enclosure was a 'gigantic necropolis, constructed for the exposure of the cadaveric remains of a large population'.

The defensive outworks at Hambledon were investigated in the southern section of the hill where a two-acre (0.8ha) enclosure, known as the Stepleton enclosure, abutted on the earthworks. Two sides of this enclosure were guarded by the treble ditches of the outworks while a single causewayed ditch guarded its other sides. It was apparently used for domestic rather than ritual purposes and traces of dwellings, wheat cultivation and the keeping of dairy cattle were found. On the inner lip of the outwork ditch evidence of a 'box rampart' built of earth contained by a timber framework was discovered, such ramparts previously having been thought to belong to much later prehistoric periods. Outworks defended the whole of the hilltop, guarding an area twice as large as that at the famous Iron Age fortress of Maiden Castle, in the same county. About 330 feet (100m) of rampart were excavated and everywhere there were signs of burning, revealing that the great fortified centre had, in the words of Dr Mercer, 'met a violent end of positively Wagnerian proportions'.

This staggering Neolithic centre was a religious focus of great importance and might have been used as a protective compound for scores of cattle. Human heads were displayed here in various places and we cannot know if they had belonged to enemies, sacrificial victims or people who met less violent deaths. The great and puzzling complex of monuments was ringed by defensive ditches, several miles of rampart composed of chalk rubble buttressed by wooden hurdles and more than 20,000 massive posts. After being successfully stormed, when some at least of the occupants and defenders were slain, the ramparts were slighted and the site was abandoned.

The excavator of Hambledon Hill also explored Carn Brea, near Redruth in Cornwall. This was a Neolithic hilltop village protected by a massive defensive wall of granite stones and boulders. Built around 3700 BC, the wall linked outcrops of rock and enclosed over 8000 square yards (7000m^2) of hilltop. Within the wall was a settlement of 150 to 200 peasant farmers and traders who exchanged locally-made greenstone axes for flint and pottery. Around 3400 BC the village was stormed and excavations have revealed almost 1000 of the attackers' flint arrowheads scattered across the site.

Until factual discoveries restricted the freedom to speculate, the Neolithic period was generally regarded as a rather idyllic age of colonising and innocence. Now it takes on a different aura coloured by intense and violent rivalries, which might best be regarded as tribal conflicts. There were great and heavily defended religious and gathering centres such as Crickley Hill and Hambledon Hill and fortified hilltop villages which extended control across the surrounding countryside. Each of the tribal foci and strongholds described perished as the result of a large-scale assault and each was then abandoned before being reoccupied and new defences established in a later and much troubled prehistoric era. Quite frequently war wounds have been discovered during investigations of Neolithic skeletal remains and it is clear that conflict and the threat of battle have existed in Britain for well over 5000 years. Many more Neolithic strongholds doubtless await recognition, while others are suspected and await excavation. It now seems probable that many of the great hillforts of the Iron Age stand upon or within the remains of strongholds which are two or three thousand years older.

During the Bronze Age (c. 2500–650 BC) society appears to have become both more stratified and more unsettled. Excavations have revealed the bronze weapons and gold trinkets of the warrior and aristocratic élites, yet at the same time a worsening climate brought the desertion of many upland territories. Some of the strongholds which evolved were apparently the fortified 'palaces' of chieftains or nobles, while others were the precursors and the prototypes of the hillforts of the Iron Age. In addition there were homesteads and small villages which, while seemingly of a domestic nature, were built on artificial islands surrounded by the waters of lakes or meres. Of the fortified palaces or 'mini-hillforts' of the Bronze Age the best-known examples are near Thwing in the Yorkshire Wolds and Springfield Lyons in Essex. At Thwing, a circular ditch some 10 feet (3m) deep enclosed an area about 120 yards (108m) in diameter; inside the ditch was a rampart and inside this, a second ditch. At the centre of the enclosure was a circular arrangement of posts, perhaps an open circle or the supports of a gigantic roof. Initially the fort appears to have sheltered a community of farmers but later it became a focus for ritual and for the payment of tribute, with animals being driven in in large numbers for slaughter, presumably at the behest of a resident chieftain who extended his control over a surrounding estate. The Thwing fort has been dated to the years around 1000 BC. The 'prince's stronghold' at Springfield Lyons was built about a century later. Here six entrance causeways, the main one guarded by an elaborate gateway, breached the outer moat, ramparts and timber palisade. The fortified enclosure was 213 feet (65m) in diameter and accommodated a group of circular thatch-roofed buildings. The main dwelling had an elaborate porchway facing towards the main entrance and was apparently the abode of the resident chieftain.

'Crannogs' are artificial islands of brushwood, stakes and rubble which were built to carry dwellings. They first appeared during the Bronze Age, others were built in the Iron Age and Roman periods and some British crannogs continued to be occupied in the Dark Ages, while in Ireland crannog life continued through the Middle Ages and even beyond. Some Scottish lochs and Irish loughs accommodated numerous crannog communities. When crannog sites are excavated they produce unspectacular relics of peasant life and do not appear to have been the abodes of chieftains or warriors. Although certain Irish crannogs were defended as late as the seventeenth century, it is not clear how far thoughts of defence influenced the adoption of crannog life and how far the choice was guided by convenience for fishing and canoe travel.

One of the most exciting recent archaeological discoveries took place at Flag Fen on the eastern outskirts of Peterborough in 1982. Here, in the late Bronze Age, a massive artificial platform of stakes and branches covering an area of around 2.5 acres (c. 1ha) was built in the fenland. The excavation of the site may continue into the next century but it seems that the timber platform may have supported around ten enormous wooden longhouses. At first it was thought that the masses of timbers preserved in the waterlogged peaty ground represented the remains of some gigantic water-girt stronghold but now it appears that the rise in water level occurred gradually during the occupation of the platform and that the settlement was more domestic than military in function.

Neolithic fortresses, like Crickley Hill and Hambledon Hill, are difficult for the modern mind to comprehend because they embody an array of religious, ritualistic, military and economic functions. They were tribal capitals of a kind but no single word in our vocabulary can describe them. Hillforts were until quite recently regarded as the hilltop fortresses of the Iron Age, but now it is clear that they began to be built in the Bronze Age and could have developed gradually from both domestic settlements and religious sites. At Rams Hill, on the Berkshire Downs, a hilltop enclosure dominated an area rich in burials; then a massive palisade of posts set in a deep trench was built around 1200 BC to embrace an oval space about 10,800 sq yards (9000 sq m) in area. A dog was buried in the bottom of one of the holes dug to hold the posts which flanked the entrance passageway. Subsequently a flat-bottomed ditch was dug to enclose an area of about 2.5 acres (1ha), the rubble from the ditch being used to build a rampart breached by three entrances and faced in chalk blocks and sarsen stone boulders. The entrance defences underwent various remodellings and at one stage a sheep or a goat and a piglet were buried in holes dug to house entrance posts. Within the fortified area dwellings and buildings which may have been granaries were built. Subsequently the site was fortified by the rampart and ditch of a more conventional Iron Age hillfort.

In the centuries after 1000 BC numerous palisaded hilltop settlements developed in Southern Britain and in the years following about 750 BC many of the palisades were superseded by massive earthen ramparts and ditches. The evolution of hillforts appears to have been complicated and variable. Some seem to have evolved from rather mysterious palisaded hilltop ritual sites, some from fortifications erected around pre-existing villages and others from the elaboration of meeting and trading sites. All were 'central places' for the local or regional communities, though this fashionable phrase can embrace a variety of functions. One thing is certain: as the age of bronze gradually yielded to that of iron a multitude of sites had their natural defences enormously enhanced by the construction of massive girdles of ramparts and ditches. These defenceworks were periodically improved until the imposition of Roman rule dampened down most tribal rivalries. In the part of Britain lying to the south of the Lake District and the North Yorkshire moors some 1350 hillforts were built, many of them embodying a prodigious amount of toil. Northern England and Scotland contain hundreds of additional examples.

The causes of the enthusiasm for hillfort construction may have been rooted both in the environment and in society. After around 1300 BC the climate of Britain began to deteriorate and the trickle of refugees from the sodden uplands and waterlogged clay vales must have increased tensions in countrysides which were heavily populated by peasant communities. In addition, society was progressively becoming more stratified and weapons increasingly more formidable, so that communities might either have looked to chieftains and their warrior retainers for protection or else have been subjugated and controlled by such people. Recently, however, some archaeologists have emphasised the non-military aspects of hillforts. The excavation of hillfort interiors has frequently revealed not only the characteristic circular dwellings of the period but also rectangular structures supported by posts at their four corners. These 'four posters' are most usually interpreted as granaries and thus the hillforts containing them emerge as fortified grain stores. It is significant that two 'four posters' excavated at Crickley Hill were found to have been full of barley when they burned down. Perhaps the communities stored their precious seed corn or part of their harvest in their local hillfort, or perhaps chieftains extracted a tribute in grain from the surrounding countryside and traded it or redistributed it as a form of largesse.

The hillfort would always have been closely associated with the surrounding countryside and the people living there. In some senses at least it would have served as a local or regional capital. Archaeologists engaged in the recent excavation of Caer Cadwgan hillfort in the Teifi valley of South-West Wales noted that the commanding position of the fort in relation to the present parish hinted that the parish could have evolved from the old hillfort territory. They also found that the fort stood at the boundary zone between the valley ploughlands and the upland grazings. In late medieval times shepherds and graziers built their summer huts in this boundary zone and there is speculation that the Iron Age hillfort may have accommodated a similar kind of summertime population. At the time of the Roman conquest in A D 43 Britain was divided into various tribal territories, each as large as or larger than a modern county. The more progressive of the southern tribes had established tribal capitals, generally lowland sites defended by outworks. No hillfort can have commanded an area as extensive as a tribal territory but it is quite possible that hillfort-centred districts were the sub-divisions of such territories.

Most of the earlier hillfort excavations consisted of sectioning selected portions of ramparts. Although such efforts produced much evidence about prehistoric military engineering, it was later appreciated that what was being defended was likely to be more interesting than the defences themselves. However the painstaking exploration of a hillfort interior is a mammoth task. At the medium-sized Hampshire hillfort of Danebury the digging began in 1969 and as yet only half of the interior has been exposed. In 1979 another ambitious excavation was launched at Hengistbury Head hillfort on the Dorset coast and it has produced evidence that the associated harbour lay on a major trade route to the Mediterranean; after 100 BC the trade was vitalised by Roman entrepreneurs based in the south of Gaul. Wine, glass and figs were imported in exchange for raw materials, grain and slaves. It is less easy to discover how far trade featured in the roles of more typical inland hillforts, although the commanding enclosures with their prominent situations would seem to have been the natural venues for markets and fairs.

A great many hillforts contained settlements, and these places might be compared to the defensive hilltop medieval villages of some Continental countries. At sites such as Hod Hill and Maiden Castle in Dorset these settlements developed into virtual towns. However, whereas the houses found on the Continent tend to have been rectangular or barrack-like buildings, in Britain the houses were almost invariably circular, suggesting that the hillfort villages were a native rather than an imported phenomenon. Crickley Hill is an exception. The Iron Age buildings were aisled halls – long buildings with their roofs carried on internal posts which defined aisles – similar to some Continental buildings of the period. Apart from the conventional dwellings there are the 'four posters' mentioned earlier. As well as granaries, these have variously been regarded as watch towers or rectangular dwellings on stilts. Hillforts also contained many grain storage pits, which could be sealed in such a way that the stored grain would not rot or germinate for months or even years. What such communities generally lacked was easy access to water and this was the main drawback of hilltop life. Usually, however, a source of water could be found within half a mile or so of the fort.

Hillfort defences were of various kinds. Once built they had to be maintained and renovated and periodically they might be improved or completely redesigned. Ramparts, ditches, walls and palisades embodied a phenomenal amount of toil and whole communities must have been conscripted for construction work for periods of months or even years. In essence the builders of hillforts forced their enemies to launch their attacks across deep ditches backed by steep earthen ramparts or walls. The earliest hillfort defences were palisades of upright timber posts which might have evolved from post rings encircling Bronze Age ritual sites. Subsequently the palisade posts might be set in earth and rubble excavated from a ditch which fronted the timber defences. At around 650 BC, at the start of the Iron Age (650 BC–AD 43), such palisaded hilltop settlements could have been quite numerous. As the hillforts developed, timber was used to stabilise and reinforce ramparts which superseded the palisade concept. Box ramparts were built which consisted of an inner and outer ring of timber uprights linked together by horizontal posts, the space between the rings being packed with earth, stones and boulders excavated from a massive ditch just outside the outer post ring. A ramp of earth might also be built behind the inner ring of posts to enable defenders to rush to the top of their rampart when danger threatened. Some forts with box ramparts were built in the Bronze Age, like the Rams Hill example mentioned above.

In Scotland, where glaciers had scoured most hills clear of soil, ramparts tended to be built of stone rubble which was stabilised by a framework of lacing timbers. Many of these Scottish hillforts are 'vitrified', the lacing timbers having been ignited to generate such an inferno that sections of the stone ramparts were turned to glass. If vitrification improved the quality of the defences its use would easily be explained – but it did not. The vitrified forts of Scotland remain a major archaeological puzzle. One may only imagine that after the capture of a fort with timber-laced stone ramparts the victors may have heaped brushwood around the ramparts and burned it to produce enough heat to fire the lacing timbers and vitrify the stone. Why they would want to do this cannot be explained, unless it formed part of a ritual of conquest.

In due course the box rampart was simplified by dispensing with the inner ring of posts while an outer ring was built to retain a sloping rampart of soil piled up behind its posts. Further simplification after approximately 350 BC produced the 'glacis' rampart in which soil was piled up on the inner side of the fronting ditch so that attackers emerging from the ditch had to surmount a continuous steep and greasy slope. The most striking example of such ramparts can be seen at Maiden Castle in Dorset, where the sharp slope from ditch bottom to rampart crest involved an ascent of more than 80 feet (25m). Glacis ramparts are still imposing features at many English hillforts but in the uplands of Scotland and Wales ramparts of drystone walling were built of materials gathered from scree or quarried from rock-cut ditches. The most impressive of such hillfort walls can be seen at Tre'r Ceiri fort on the Lleyn peninsula of North Wales, where sections of walling more than 12 feet (4m) tall still survive, along with the ruins of many contemporary dwellings.

The evolution of hillfort defences culminated during the last century or so of independent Celtic rule, with the imitation of the 'Fécamp'-style defences of Gaul, involving the excavation of wide, steep-sided and flat-bottomed ditches in place of the earlier 'U'- or 'V'- shaped ditches. Such ditches are found in Southern England and might have been inspired by fears of Roman invasion. In general, however, the building of a hillfort was a massive undertaking more likely to be countenanced in times of peace than when attacks were imminent. Excavations show that defences gradually became slumped and degraded by erosion. Periodically repair work or 'modernisation' would take place, possibly when new tensions erupted or else to impress neighbours or outsiders with the scale or impregnability of one's stronghold. The redevelopment of a hillfort could involve more work than the original building operations, with the construction of a new outer ring of banks and ditches to convert a 'univallate' fort into a 'bivallate' one or the creation of more than two rings to produce a 'multivallate' fort, like Clovelly Dykes in Devon.

The weak points of any fortress are likely to be its entrances and the hillfort communities demonstrated ingenuity in their attempts to fortify the approaches to gateways. Sometimes the entrance was a gap in the ramparts reached via a causeway across the fronting ditch, but unless such an entrance could be heavily defended and blocked in the event of attack it would become the focus for any assault. In some cases the entrance was guarded by earthen outworks from which defenders could attack the flanks of any party advancing to batter down the gates. These outworks could take the form of projecting horns but in a few cases, like Danebury or Maiden Castle, they formed a virtual maze of banks and ditches within which enemy forces might be annihilated before ever reaching the entrance. Guard chambers could be established in recesses in the hornwork, beside the gateway, or in the entrance passage passing through the ramparts. The timber work associated with entrance defences has perished and can only be deduced from excavated evidence of post-holes. Gateposts, which must have supported heavy timber gates, are often recognisable and there might well have been walkways and watch towers above the gates. Slings and slingstones provided the main defensive armament and forces of slingers will have been stationed at key points around the entrance and along the ramparts. The attention and ingenuity displayed in Iron Age military engineering show that the builders of hillforts expected their defences to be put to the test.

Finally, it is vital to recognise the great variation found within this class of strongholds. In terms of size the range is immense and runs from Stanwick fort in North Yorkshire, with its four miles (6.4km) of outer ramparts and 850-acre (340ha) interior, to scores of little forts where walls or ditches enclosed less than an acre of ground. In some situations, like those of the cliff castles of the southern and western seaboard, the terrain was so favourable that only short lengths of bank and ditch were needed to guard the neck of a sea-girt promontory, while in other places, like Badbury Rings in Dorset, elaborate earthworks were slung around ground of modest natural defensive potential. Forts crowned lofty hills, like Ingle-borough in the Yorkshire Pennines, and mini-mountains, like Bennachie in North-East Scotland, but were also constructed on slopes, plateaux, headlands, valleys and even coastal plains – Holkham fort in Norfolk was built on an island in a tidal salt marsh. Apart from the Scottish examples, the forts tend to be concentrated in Wessex, South-Western England and Wales, with a multitude of small forts being found in Cornwall and Pembrokeshire. A broad band of hillforts of various sizes spans the border lands of England and Wales, which suggests it was turbulent marshland in prehis-toric times. The forts are much fewer in the English lands to the north and east of a line joining the Mersey and Thames estuary, where many promising hillocks were undefended. Many hillforts in the English lowlands have doubtless been destroyed by ploughing; even so the distribution patterns suggest that the political realities differed from one region to another. In the west the hillfort seems to have been thought essential to the existence of the community, while elsewhere mobile forces of infantry and charioteers may have settled their conflicts in open warfare.

Each major tribal territory incorporated several or dozens of hillforts. It is conceivable that some territories may have been dominated by a 'paramount' hillfort capital, but in the more progressive territories of the south and south-east, defended, semi-urban tribal capitals or *oppida* were established during the first century BC, such as those near Colchester and St Albans. Most hillforts must have been governed by a tribal sub-chief or local patriarch, and on the plains below the ramparts one could expect to find landowners living in the prehistoric equivalents of the moated homesteads of the Middle Ages or tower houses of the centuries which followed: private strongholds with the capability to resist small-scale attacks. Villages were not particularly common and the majority of people lived in hamlets and farmsteads. These little settlements could be undefended or ringed by ramparts, ditches and palisades and a few examples have been excavated. The chalk knoll of Staple Howe in the Yorkshire Wolds was crowned by a single dwelling standing within a fenced enclosure. Around 500 BC this was superseded by two dwellings and a granary set in an enclosure defended by a stout palisade of upright posts reinforced by shorter posts. The Iron Age settlement now entombed by Heathrow Airport was larger and consisted of a rectangular enclosure bounded by a ditch some eight feet (2.4m) deep and a bank about ten feet (3m) high which protected eleven houses, a building interpreted as a temple or shrine and a stockpen. The bank would almost certainly have carried a timber palisade so that the settlement was well equipped for defence.

The diversity of the Iron Age fortifications tells of communities plagued by insecurity. It also suggests that the political life of the country was very complex. We cannot know why some peasants and nobles invested heavily in defences while others were content to live in 'open', undefended settlements. It is clear that conflict and treachery often dominated the relations between the major tribal groupings but the numerous hillforts found within most territories suggest that internal strife and raiding were also common. It would be easy to interpret the multitude of defenceworks as evidence of societies that were anarchic and ever at war – but such societies could never have achieved either the sustained efforts of military engineering which produced marvels such as Maiden Castle or the almost total agricultural mastery of the countryside. Perhaps it was the success of Bronze Age and Iron Age farming which allowed the population to grow to such a level that communities felt a powerful need to defend their landholdings against intruders and hungry neighbours. At this time, just as during much of the medieval period, there was no ruler strong enough to outlaw warfare and impose peace upon the countryside, though unlike the medieval situation most of the greater Iron Age strongholds were communal refuges rather than dynastic fortresses.

Some selected hillforts can now be explored in a little more detail. Hod Hill in Dorset is interesting for several reasons. It is, for example, the only case where a Roman auxiliary fort reused the native hillfort defences. Also, clear traces survive of the settlement patterns in an undisturbed section of the interior. The fort occupies a spur in the chalk scarplands of Dorset, a site enjoying the natural defences provided by very steep slopes to the west and north. Between 1951 and 1958 the site was excavated on behalf of the British Museum by Sir Ian Richmond. This work showed that at a fairly early stage in the Iron Age the spur was defended by a single rampart and ditch which outlined a roughly rectangular enclosure. The ditch was about 20 feet (6m) wide and about 10 feet (3m) deep and the material excavated from the ditch was used to build the box rampart. This rampart was revetted front and rear with timber so that the upright posts presented a continuous wall to any attacker. The rampart was strengthened and stabilised with longitudinal timbers linked to the uprights and the framework was packed with the rubble from the ditch to create a wall about 10 feet (3m) thick and of equal height.

Later in the Iron Age the box rampart was remodelled to form a glacis rampart with a continuous slope downward to the foot of the ditch. The volume of the rampart was increased by adding chalk rubble quarried from pits which were dug just behind the bank. The new rampart stood about 30 feet (9m) above the foot of the ditch and seems to have been unusual in being crowned with a parapet of flint blocks which protected defenders on the wall walk that followed the crest of the rampart. In addition a palisade was built beyond the top of the ditch. Human bones found around the base of this palisade have led to the suggestion that the bodies of enemies may have been impaled and displayed upon it. The new rampart continued all the way around the enclosure, although the box rampart which preceded it had not been considered necessary in the western sector which was guarded by an extremely steep slope. Gateways were provided near the north-eastern and south-western corners of the fort and the excavations showed that the north-eastern entrance was protected by the outer palisade, which curved in towards the gate passage. This passage was 23 feet (7m) wide and was crossed by a timber bridge supported at each end by pairs of posts, the bridge overlooking the gates.

Later still, the ditch was enlarged and the material excavated from it was used to build a counterscarp bank beyond its outer lip. This bank was about 43 feet (13m) wide and 7 to 10 feet (2 to 3m) high. The enlarged ditch was now 33 feet (10m) wide and 16 feet (5m) deep. The digging of the new ditch and bank was apparently 'consecrated' by the burial of the body of a young woman in a pit beneath the counterscarp just outside the north-eastern entrance. Whether she was a sacrificial victim is not known.

Possibly as a response to the Roman landings, the rampart was increased in width by around 10 feet (3m) and in height by about 3 feet (0.9m). The work seems to have been incomplete at the time when the Roman army appeared outside the ramparts. The invaders assaulted the hillfort community with showers of iron bolts fired from a form of giant crossbow known as a *ballista*. They concentrated their fire on a large dwelling which stood in its own compound and which was surely judged to have been the residence of the local chieftain. The excavators found eleven iron bolts which, from their angle of landing, had apparently been fired from a *ballista* stationed just outside the south-eastern angle of the fort. No skeletons of people killed during the battle for Hod Hill were found and it is possible that, awed by the Roman artillery and the possible death of their leader, the hillfort community chose to surrender.

The interior of the fort was packed with circular dwellings and must have contained a substantial community. When the fort fell the flint breastwork guarding the rampart walk was demolished and the houses of the hillfort dwellers were knocked down. The fort was commandeered by the Roman army and an auxiliary fort was built in its north-western angle, using the existing ramparts to fortify its northern and western sides, with new ramparts being built to the south and east. Timber buildings were erected within the fort, but the site was abandoned following an accidental fire

(Opposite)
The ramparts of Tencrom hillfort, Cornwall.

The ruins of the granary at Hardknott fort, Cumbria.

(Left)
The restored Norman castle overlooking Norwich.

(Opposite above)
The stone keep of Peveril Castle, Castleton, Derbyshire, with the old hillfort of Mam Tor behind.

(Opposite below)
Bodiam Castle

which seems to have occurred a few years after its capture, around AD 51.

South Cadbury Hillfort in Somerset is one of the most interesting and celebrated of the British hillforts as a result of detailed excavations accomplished by Professor L. Alcock from 1966–70. The fact that the fort was a possible candidate for the site of the legendary Camelot of the Arthurian legends also greatly helped to publicise his work. The excavations showed that the first occupation of the hill took place in Neolithic times, around 3300 BC, and a second occupation during the Bronze Age was also evident. During the Iron Age an undefended settlement was established early in the sixth century BC and in the middle of the next century the hill received its first fortification. This took the form of a modest bank which was revetted with timber and fronted by a small ditch. The defences were then neglected until around 400 BC when a new box rampart was built. The ditch was cut deeply into the limestone rock and the rampart was stabilised with a revetment of limestone slabs.

By around 200 BC South Cadbury hillfort had assumed the lay-out which can be seen today, with four lines of ramparts, all but the outermost bank being fronted by a ditch. The gateway was furnished with semicircular guard chambers and the settlement existing within the ramparts had grown to become a small town. The dwellings were of both the circular and the rectangular forms and were relatively spacious. Several were rebuilt as they fell into decay, and this suggests that occupation was continuing without interruption.

For a while the fortifications were neglected, but around the start of the first century AD they were again repaired. It is not clear whether settlement had continued into this period, but on the summit of the hill a square timber shrine with a broad veranda was erected and the bones of twenty sacrificial animals were buried in front of it. Older rectangular buildings which existed in the vicinity of this building have been interpreted as earlier shrines.

The South Cadbury fort escaped the destruction meted out to other western hillforts, like Hod Hill, by Vespasian's Roman troops in the AD 40s. But the end, when it came, between AD 70 and AD 80, was violent. On the floor of the gate passage the excavators found the remains of thirty men, women and children who had been hacked down and their bodies left to be dismembered by wild animals. It seems likely that members of the South Cadbury community had engaged in some form of disorder which was the cause

(Opposite above)
The well-preserved domestic range at Manorbier Castle.

(Opposite below)
Rhuddlan Castle.

of a merciless Roman reprisal raid. A little later Roman troops set up temporary huts in neat rows within the ramparts and began the systematical destruction of the gateway defences. For the remainder of the Roman period the hill seems to have been virtually deserted, although numerous discoveries of coins of the third and fourth centuries suggest that some forms of temple may have existed there.

After about AD 470 the hill was refortified, the new ramparts following the line of the old inner bank and faced on both sides with drystone walling. A timber aisled hall measuring 62 by 33 feet (19m × 10m) which dates from this Arthurian reoccupation of the site was excavated and it is likely that unexcavated sections of the interior were also occupied by dwellings in this unsettled period.

This was not the last period of fortification at South Cadbury, for in the reign of Ethelred the Unready (978–1013 and 1014–16) a rampart bank of earth and rubble was built and was faced with a revetment of mortared masonry. These refurbished defences against Danish invaders may have protected a projected town – the foundation trenches for a peculiar cross-shaped church were dug – but the building was never completed. Although a mint was established here the dates from the coins which were struck show that it only operated from 1009 to 1019.

Burnswark hillfort, near Dumfries, displays evidence of a quite different type of later use. On the eastern part of the summit at least, the substantial defences were preceded by a simple palisade, many of the traces of which were obliterated when the ramparts were built. Elsewhere excavation of the main rampart has revealed the traces of an earlier double palisade, built in about 500 BC and formed of close-set posts erected in rows about 10 feet (3m) apart. Later a rampart of earth and rubble which was reveted in stone on its outer face was built over the old palisade and an unrevetted outer bank was added. Finally, a bank of turf was built up to heighten the main rampart. Within these defences a settlement of circular timber dwellings developed. The hillfort was abandoned and left derelict until it was chosen to play a part in Roman military siege training concerned with practice attacks, staged to initiate the troops in the techniques used to conquer hillforts. Successive Roman forts were built on the flanks of the hill to the north-west and the south-east of the old hillfort during the second century and sling bullets were fired into the tumbling ramparts.

Promontory forts or cliff castles were extremely popular in rocky western coastal areas, where the natural configuration of the coast allowed great economies of effort to be made in the creation of strongholds. The Gurnard's Head or Trereen Dinas promontory fort on the north coast of Cornwall is a good example, for here a rampart only about 200 feet (60m) in length was sufficient to fortify a cliff-girt promontory some 7 acres (3ha) in area. As the archaeologist A. H. A. Hogg has pointed out (*Hill-Forts of Britain*, Hart Davis MacGibbon, 1975), on an inland site a bank some 1150 feet (350m) long would be needed to encircle an enclosure only 2.4 acres (1ha) in area. At Gurnard's Head, near Zennor, the rocky headland was defended by two banks and ditches. The inner rampart was the main defensive structure and consisted of a rubble wall about 10 feet (3m) wide and originally of a similar height. In front of this wall two ditches were hacked into the hard rock and a lower wall of rubble was built between the ditches. It was apparently intended to enhance these defences with an additional 'V'-shaped ditch, but this was dug only half way across the neck of the headland before being abandoned. Traces of thirteen circular dwellings have been recognised on the defended promontory and the pottery associated with them suggests that the settlement dated from the early years of the first century BC.

Chapter Two

Hadrian's Wall near
Housesteads fort.

THE ARMOUR OF EMPIRE

In AD 43 a Roman invasion force landed at Richborough in Kent and subsequently England, Wales and Southern Scotland were incorporated into the Roman empire. The conquest introduced completely new outlooks on the defensive needs of Britain, for while the hillforts of the natives had existed as local and regional communal strongholds, the Roman military creations were all part of a coherent strategy for the subjugation and retention of this island outpost of the empire. Unlike the British, who were fragmented between tribes and sub-tribes, the Romans were able to regard Britain as an entity and introduced a wide array of military engineering projects, each an integral part of a strategy of control. These included roads, marching camps, fortresses of many sizes, linear defenceworks, watch towers and, eventually, coastal defences.

Independent Britain had previously existed both as a nuisance and as a tempting fruit waiting to be plucked by any emperor anxious to boost his prestige in the imperial heartland. British tribesmen seem to have provoked unrest amongst the Celtic peoples of the Continent who were already subject to Roman occupation, and their conquest also offered control of an attractive range of agricultural products and raw materials. The Roman commanders were probably more concerned by the problems and uncertainties of the Channel crossing than by those of conquest once the invasion forces had landed. In the event, one division of the fleet landed at Richborough, one probably landed near Chichester to divide and confuse the opposition, while a third appears to have headed for the vicinity of Deal or Reculver in Kent. The British did not succeed in disrupting the landings and the decisive battle did not occur until the legions were engaged in fording the Medway. Here the battle lasted for two days and another battle was fought when the British withdrew to the Thames near London. With victory in their grasp the invaders summoned their emperor, Claudius, who arrived to harvest the plaudits of triumph. Then the invasion army divided into three forces, extending the conquest to the South-West, the Midlands and the Humber.

It appears that as the legions advanced so the British often sought refuge in the false security of their hillforts. The Romans were familiar with the tactics and engineering used to smash Continental strongholds and during Caesar's second raid on Britain in 54 BC they had attacked the fortified capital of the Trinovantes tribe at St Albans. In his account of the Gallic wars Caesar wrote:

The Britons apply the name of stronghold to any woodland spot, difficult of access and fortified with a rampart and ditch, to which they are in the habit of resorting in order to escape a hostile raid. Caesar . . . found that the place was of great natural strength and well fortified; nevertheless he proceeded to assault it on two sides. The enemy stood their ground a short time, but could not sustain the onset of our infantry, and fled precipitately from another part of the stronghold. A great quantity of cattle was found in the place, and many of the garrison were captured as they were trying to escape, and killed.

Julius Caesar, *The Battle for Gaul*

Ninety years later more than twenty 'towns' or hillforts fell as the Second Legion, under Vespasian, advanced into Wessex. The Hod Hill fort was conquered after a Roman artillery barrage and Maiden Castle fell when the Roman infantry stormed its eastern entrance. At Spetisbury Rings fort near Blandford Forum the bodies of around 120 defenders were entombed in the ditch of their stronghold; at Hod Hill an infantry and cavalry fort was established in a corner of the Iron Age enclosure while the surviving inhabitants of the Poundbury and Maiden Castle forts were re-settled in Dorchester and those from the Wrekin were removed to Wroxeter.

The subjugation of Britain did not pose any great new problems for the legions and, as in other parts of the empire, the advance of Roman civilisation was carried on an integrated and well-engineered system of roads. Much later the British would apply military roads to the pacification of the Scottish Highlands and railways served a similar purpose in Ireland and the empire beyond the seas. While they later gained great economic importance, the Roman roads were as indispensable to the conquest and policing of Britain as the forts were. They were largely built by the military, with foundations of stone or clay, coated in layers of rammed gravel. Sometimes a surface of cobbles or stone slabs was added. Stone kerbs lined the sides of the roads and flanking ditches protected the foundations from waterlogging. The network radiated outwards from London, which was well placed to serve as a link between the island colony and the mainland empire. This road system provided the framework for all that followed, thus establishing London's predominance in the affairs of the country. The roads headed unerringly towards their destinations, linking up the chains of vantage points adopted by the surveyors. Where possible the alignments were straight, and even curves were generally composed of a sequence of short, straight sections, while the surveyors also sought to attain higher ground and then to follow the higher levels wherever possible.

When advancing into unknown and potentially hostile territory the soldiers always sought to build temporary marching camps before becoming benighted and vulnerable to attack. These camps were built according to standardised plans, with the rounded corners of the playing-card shaped plan allowing more troops to be concentrated to resist attacks on the angles of the camp. Ramparts, about the height of a man, were of earthen upcast from the 'V'-shaped fronting ditch and each trooper carried a brace of pointed stakes which were hammered into the crest of the bank to form a palisade. Entrances, normally set at the mid-points of the sides of the camp, were defended by a length of bank and ditch placed in front of the gap or by extending the rampart and ditch defences to sweep around the gap so that headlong assaults on the entrances were impossible. Such temporary camps might be abandoned after just one night of occupation, be developed to house more permanent garrisons or grow into formidable fortresses, like the one at York.

Original plans for the invasion may only have envisaged the conquest of the territory of the Catuvellauni in South-Eastern England and the encirclement of the territory by a buffer zone of client kingdoms. With this achieved and the legions advancing north and west, the Romans may have sought no more than the domination of the lowland zone of England, but with the absence in most places of clear-cut defensible natural frontiers the troops were drawn further and further into the uplands. Here native life continued much as before; minerals, such as lead and gold, were mined but the main Roman effort was devoted to policing, necessary to keep the arteries of empire open and to prevent local revolts from spilling over into the productive civil zone. Garrison posts were established beside the roads, one of the most interesting survivals being Hardknott Castle in Cumbria, which guarded the Hardknott Pass at the head of Eskdale. It was built less than a century after the Roman landings and garrisoned – to their disgust, one might imagine – by troops recruited in sunny Yugoslavia. Walled in roughly squared stone and containing barracks, a headquarters building, granary and commanding officer's house, the fort had

baths just outside its walls and a parade ground partly hacked into
the slopes to provide a suitably level area nearby. Drilling at a
height of 800 feet (245m) with winds blasting in from the grey
Atlantic must have inspired homesickness in many a trooper's
heart, but at least the hot baths kindled reminders of civilisation.

The walls of Hardknott fort.

For some years the armies probed and buttressed the margins of
the empire. In AD 60 the Romans launched an assault across the
Menai Straits on Anglesey, a bastion of Celtic religious fanaticism,
but events on the frontier were overtaken by the violent uprising of

the Iceni of Norfolk under Boudicca. Both London and Verulamium (St Albans) were sacked by the insurgents before peace was restored. In AD 79 governor Julius Agricola completed the reconquest of Wales and then led his forces into Southern Scotland as far as the Tay. For many years to come, however, Roman policy seems to have vacillated on the question of where imperial expansion should end. Around AD 82 Agricola seems to have contemplated the invasion of Ireland, but the question of whether the whole of Scotland was worth the effort needed to conquer and pacify it remained unresolved. He launched a great invasion of Northern Scotland and a massive victory was achieved at an unidentified site in the North-East. The marching camps of this invasion have been recognised as far north as Aberdeen and the legions seem almost to have reached the Moray Firth.

The Roman commanders will have seen enough of the Highlands, Grampians and Cairngorms to realise that the terrain might have been made for guerrilla warfare. Armies withdrew southwards and work on a great fortress at Inchtuthil near Dunkeld was begun. Other forts were built to command the mouths of the glens and prevent outpourings of rebel forces from the hills beyond. Soon, however, the strongholds were abandoned and attempts were made to fortify a line marked by the road from Falkirk to the Tay by establishing a chain of watch towers. Already the Romans were turning to the concept of a fixed imperial frontier enforced by linear defenceworks. About AD 90 there was another withdrawal, this time to a zone roughly corresponding with the present Anglo-Scottish border, while a decade or so later the forces were moved back to the narrow belt of country between the Solway and the Tyne. This time the notion of a linear frontierwork was rejected in favour of establishing a pattern of strongpoints – the Stanegate system of fortresses. The fortresses were supported by roads and set up at intervals of a day's march, then supplemented by 'half-day' forts. The paved road of Stanegate running from Carlisle to Corbridge gave the system some coherence and the major forts were at Chesterholm, Corbridge and Nether Denton.

In AD 122 Emperor Hadrian visited Britain. He will have known of the inability of the Stanegate system to prevent cross-border movements by tribesmen and have been influenced by the notion that that which could not be included should be excluded (as manifested, for example, by the Great Wall of China and the Roman frontierworks in the Rhineland). Such factors argued for the establishment of a great cross-country barrier: Hadrian's Wall. For much of the length of the wall the builders were able to exploit the natural advantages of the Whin Sill, a sheet of volcanic rock which presented a cliff-like edge towards the north.

From the River Irthing westwards to the Solway the wall was built of earth and turf, but from the Irthing to Newcastle it was of squared stone, about 10 feet (3m) thick and half as high again. Whenever the geology allowed it was fronted by a ditch, while at intervals of about a mile there were gatehouses with small garrisons and between pairs of these 'milecastles' two regularly spaced turrets served as watch towers. The turrets and milecastles did not end with the wall but continued down the coast to guard against invasion from the west and seaborne outflanking movements from the north. Originally the wall was intended as a forward barrier which was supported by troops from the Stanegate forts, but soon these were abandoned and the garrisons moved up to man the wall. Twelve new forts were established on the wall, the one at Housesteads, with its typical 'playing-card' form, east and west gatehouses, angle towers, headquarters building, granaries and hospital being a popular tourist attraction today. The final stages in the building of the wall included its extention eastwards at a narrower width and, around AD 130, the excavation of the Vallum, a great ditch running to the south of the wall which defined the frontier and customs zone that contained the barrier.

The great enterprise had only been completed for about a decade when the armies advanced again into Scotland. Hadrian had enjoyed the prestige of building the wall; but now his successor, Antoninus Pius, needed his own kudos. And so a wall was built across the isthmus between the Forth and the Clyde. The Antonine Wall was a cut-price job built of turf on a rubble bed rather than of stone, crowned by a timber breastwork and fronted by a ditch. Despite its less imposing aspect (and generally unimposing condition today) this wall carried a garrison of up to 7000 men, twice that of Hadrian's Wall, and fortresses were built at roughly two-mile intervals. Milecastles were also provided and there were probably also watch towers at intervals of about 300 yards (275m) and platforms for beacons were placed in suitable places. Fortlets guarded the roads running northwards to supply the wall garrison. This frontierwork did not endure for long after the death of its sponsor and in AD 161 troops were withdrawn to the stone wall, though four outpost forts in the border country north of Hadrian's

Wall were manned to preserve a Roman presence and give early warning of unrest amongst the tribesmen.

Behind the shield of the northern frontierworks the Roman troops were dispersed in more than 250 forts, some of them massive and extensive, like the ones which stimulated the growth of towns at York and Lincoln, others humble garrison posts. Normally these followed the well-established playing-card plan, each with its principal entrance set in one of the short sides and subsidiary entrances in the other sides. Inside the fort the streets formed a neat grid-work, with the headquarters building being set at a 'T'-junction facing the main entrance, the commander's residence to one side of it and granaries containing sufficient provisions to supply the garrison for a year on the other. Much of the interior of the fort was occupied by barracks blocks – timber buildings on stone footings which were equipped with verandas where troopers would take their meals and tend to their equipment. Special quarters for the centurion projected from the end of each block. Other buildings included the hospital, workshops, bath house and latrines, while in the space between the main entrance and the headquarters building there was an open courtyard which served as an assembly and briefing area. The focus for any last-ditch fighting would be the chapel in the headquarters building which held the military standards and the funds and paychest in an underground strongroom.

The great legionary fortress at Caerleon, near Newport, covered 50 acres (20ha) and was heavily garrisoned between AD 75 and 120. It was furnished with its own amphitheatre which could seat the entire garrison of 6000 men and would double as a parade ground. Even larger was the fortress at Chester, covering 60 acres and with an amphitheatre accommodating 800 men. An amphitheatre was a considerable status symbol; the only auxiliary fort to have one was the remote station of Tomen-y-Mur, high in the hills near Ffestiniog, where it may have been awarded as a consolation for service in such a bleak setting.

By the end of the first century AD the massive legionary fortresses at Caerleon, Chester and York guarded the frontier between the settled and productive lowland zone and the potentially dangerous upland zone. In the upland zone a strong military presence was maintained throughout the occupation. The whole of Wales was conquered and the large auxiliary fort guarding the Menai Strait at Caernarvon was garrisoned from AD 78 until late in the fourth century.

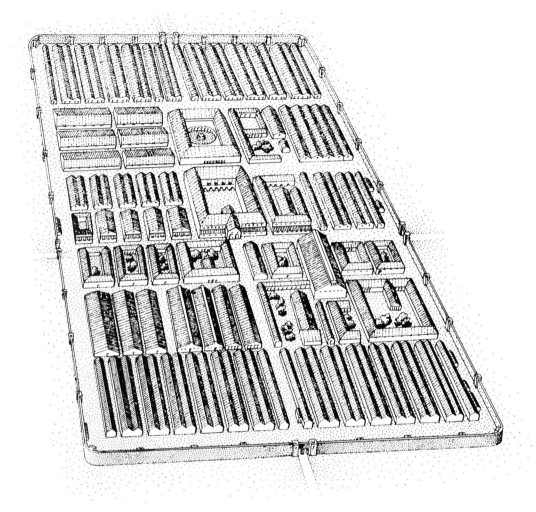

The great legionary fortresses were deliberately sited on navigable rivers, enabling them to be maintained by the fleet. The fleet was based at Dover, where one of the lighthouses, later redeveloped as a medieval church tower, survives. During the early part of the occupation the fleet was largely concerned with ferrying supplies to support land forces campaigning in the north. A large supply depot was built at South Shields and others were established on the eastern coast of Scotland. During the third century, however, the fleet developed a more active role. Within the imperial frontiers Britain was largely pacified and the native population of the lowland zone was becoming increasingly Romanised. Meanwhile pressure from seaborne barbarian raiders from the

A Roman legionary fortress, loosely based on Caerleon in South Wales.

north, Ireland and Northern Europe was increasing. The south-eastern coast of England was proving particularly vulnerable to attacks from the Continent and a chain of coastal 'forts of the Saxon shore' was established.

Around AD 286 the chain was completed and ran from Brancaster on the north Norfolk coast to Carisbrooke on the Isle of Wight via Burgh Castle, Walton Castle, Bradwell, Reculver, Richborough, Dover, Lympne, Pevensey and Porchester. By this time Rome's military involvement with Britain had passed through several stages. What may have begun as a diplomatic adventure to establish a presence in South-East England became a quest for defensible imperial frontiers. Then, as lowland England responded to the Roman occupation, it became a valuable economic component of the empire, peopled by folk who sought to preserve their stake in the system which had bought peace, prosperity and unprecedented economic expansion. This indispensable section of Roman world had to be defended against outsiders.

Burgh Castle was built around 275 and manned until the last days of the empire in Britain. It was begun as a rectangular walled enclosure measuring 640 feet by 300 feet (195m by 90m) with its walls of brick and flint rising to a height of around 15 feet (4.5m). The walls had only reached half their full height when orders were changed and solid bastions were added at intervals as the platforms for artillery pieces, the *ballistae*. The fort occupied a bluff overlooking the River Waveney and below the west wall there was a quay, enabling it to be supplied by sea.

Elsewhere the evolution was more complex. The story of Rome's association with Britain is epitomised by Richborough, in Kent. This was an invasion bridgehead guarded by ditches and a few decades after the invasion a gigantic triumphal arch was erected here. Early in the third century it was stripped of its statues and finery and a 90 foot (27m) tall signal tower was established, with the triple ditches around the podium of the arch serving as defences for the tower, the shops of the small town which had grown around the arch having been swept away. Then the ditches were filled and a great shore fort with massive flint and brick walls guarded by deep outer ditches was built, marking a further intensification of the threat of Saxon raiding. The shore forts were quite different in appearance from the earlier and somewhat stereotyped forts with their playing-card lay-outs. Although intended as bases for land and sea attacks upon invaders and pirates, they were also built to

serve as impregnable strongholds. With their lofty stone walls (30 feet [9m] high in the fort at Pevensey) and projecting artillery bastions, they superficially resembled medieval castles.

One of the corner artillery bastions at Burgh Castle. The walls are built of alternate layers of flint and brick.

The collapse of Roman power in Britain did not result from a defeat by the barbarian invaders but from decay within. Stresses elsewhere in the empire periodically led to the withdrawal of troops, which left garrisons abandoned or undermanned. The inability to conquer the whole of the British Isles exposed the Romanised territory to raids by Picts from the north and Scots from Ireland. Normally the Saxon, Pictish and Scottish assaults were not co-ordinated but in A D 367 a great barbarian conspiracy aided by a

betrayal by the scouts on the northern frontier resulted in Hadrian's Wall being overrun and Saxon assaults on Southern England and Gaul. Although the invaded territory was recovered the weaknesses within the empire could not be patched. Complex economic problems, coupled with high taxes, weakened the empire as a whole. In Britain most towns fell into decline during the second half of the occupation, although the gradual decay of urban life was paralleled by a late flowering of economic activity in the countrysides, where Romanised farms or villas flourished. Political intrigues and divisions also sapped the strength and unity of the empire – most notably between AD 286 and 293 when Carausius, the commander of the fleet in the English Channel, took unilateral control of his sphere of influence and, almost a century later, when the army chief in Britain, Magnus Maximus, seized the western provinces of the empire and depleted the British garrisons while attempting to enforce his claim to the imperial throne.

Almost to the end, however, Roman troops struggled to maintain their grip on British territory. Early in the fourth century new shore forts were built at Cardiff and Lancaster to face the challenge of barbarian raids from the Irish Sea. Some strongholds were refurbished while others lapsed into dereliction. During the twilight of Roman rule civilised life acquired a frightening dimension as unpredictable barbarian raids penetrated deeply into the heartlands of the province. Such threats were met in a manner which would have been viewed with disdain by the earlier commanders of the seemingly invincible armies. Some linear earthworks consisting of long earthen banks fronted by ditches were hastily cast up across invasion routes. Dozens of these obstacles exist in Britain and they are difficult to date by archaeological methods, but the Bokerley Dyke on the Dorset-Wiltshire boundary appears to be a late-Roman defence against attacks from the north-east. In their fear and desperation local communities even resorted to the hasty refurbishment of derelict hillforts. But the sun finally set on Roman rule in Britain at the start of the fifth century when the indigenous dignitaries faced the fact that Rome could no longer buttress their civilisation. With barbarians threatening on almost every side and foreign

Remains of the Roman fort
of the Saxon Shore at
Richborough.

mercenaries guarding the invasion routes, in AD 410 Emperor Honorius urged the Romanised British to look out for themselves as best they could.

In the military zone of the uplands the impact of Roman rule was much lighter. Traditional life and culture endured and hillforts, such as Tre'r Ceiri in Gwynedd, continued to be inhabited so long as they did not seriously challenge the forces of occupation. Far beyond the Roman frontiers strongholds appeared in a form which was new and sophisticated and yet which erupted leaving scarcely any clues to their evolution. The brochs are in some ways comparable to the much later tower houses of Scotland and Ireland – small fortresses occupied by members of a local aristocracy against attack by their neighbours. They had the form of cylindrical, slightly tapering towers up to 50 feet (18m) in height. Above their solid foundations the skilfully constructed drystone walls had an inner and an outer skin and in the space between these walls a series of chambers and galleries were created. There were no windows and access was gained via a small, barred wooden door opening into an entrance passage often furnished with guard chambers. In the hollow core of the broch a scarcement supporting a wooden veranda encircled the walls at a height of 5 to 10 feet (1.5 to 3m) above the floor level and the veranda could only be reached by scaling a stairway which exposed the unshielded side of an invader to the missiles of the defenders. No broch survives in its entirety but it is likely that the tops of the towers were equipped with sentry walks and were partially roofed.

The brochs seem to have first appeared in the first century BC and to have been built and occupied for the following two or three centuries. (As late as the Viking period the broch on Mousa in the Orkneys was successfully defended against seaborne raiders.) More than 500 examples existed and they were concentrated mainly in coastal locations in the north and west of Scotland, although a few examples were built in Southern Scotland. Orkney and Caithness have the greatest densities and were possibly the core areas from which the concept was exported.

Heavily fortified round houses or 'protobrochs' dating back as far as 600 BC may have begun the pedigree of the broch, while the compact and thickly walled Scottish Iron Age homesteads known as 'duns' must have had some evolutionary role to play. Some of these duns had galleries incorporated into their lower walls which echo the wall galleries of the brochs. However the 'galleried duns' which were regarded as the ancestor of brochs now appear to have been their contemporaries. The standardisation of broch design, the suggestion that the thick curving and tapering drystone walls could only have been built by professional broch-builders and the overall refinement of the design all pose challenges to our under-standing. Although the brochs may conceivably have been encour-aged by the threat of far-ranging Roman slave raiders, it seems that on the whole they were a response to the turbulence and uncer-tainty of life within and between the communities living in hostile and limited environments far beyond the marches of the empire.

Chapter Three

*Wareham was founded as
a Saxon fortress-town or*
burh.

Dark Age Defences

At least the withdrawal of the Roman legions and fleet clarified matters for the British: they could either maintain their own defences or expect to perish. The first step in creating an effective defensive system involved the establishment of a strong and unified government. Although the onslaught of barbarian raiders was controlled for some time the objective of unity was never achieved.

The Roman occupation had lasted for almost four centuries, and while it led to the Romanisation of a substantial part of British society it also caused its military skills to atrophy. The Romans had employed Anglo-Saxon mercenaries to resist the raids and invasions of their countrymen and the independent British leaders perpetuated the policies of converting North Sea poachers into gamekeepers. These mercenaries were probably regarded as uncouth pagan barbarians by their paymasters and they were generally billeted away from the productive lands and 'desirable' neighbourhoods. One garrison may have been established in the old hillfort at Highdown in West Sussex, where a fifth-century Saxon cemetery has been excavated.

The emergence of domestic usurpers and the penetration of the former Roman territory by bands of desperadoes heralded the age of Arthur. He was certainly not a king and is only marginally credible as an actual historical figure. Rather, he emerges dimly as a field commander who championed the cause of Romanised civilisation. There was no Camelot with battlemented walls and lofty turrets and even the loci of the legendary Arthurian battles are disputed. When we look at the legacy of monuments to this myth-ridden age we find very little and what we do find does not reveal an heroic era of castle-building but rather a modest selection of 'Dad's Army' defenceworks and an impression of local despots and patriarchs struggling to keep their heads above the waves of uncertainty.

Several old hillforts were rehabilitated and at Brent Knoll in Somerset and South Cadbury in the same county the decaying ramparts were restored. Interest in the old hilltop strongholds had revived during the third century AD, although this revival seems to have been stimulated more by the mystical attractions of the decaying foci of Iron Age life than by any pressing defensive issues. In the fourth century a trio of Gloucestershire hillforts, Lydney, Norbury and Ring Hill, was revived, with a temple to the pagan god Nodens being created at Maiden Castle. In the west some small forts were redeveloped, perhaps even founded, as the strongholds of local patriarchs. At Castle Dore near Fowey in Cornwall, archaeologists may have exposed the palace of King Mark, father of Tristan of the Tristan and Iseult legends, inside the double ramparts and ditches of the small Iron Age fort. Chun Castle in the far west of Cornwall is a circular fort guarded by two rings of walls and an outer ditch, and excavation revealed a reoccupation in the second half of the Dark Ages. Dinas Emrys hillfort, standing on a rocky hillock near Beddgelert in North Wales, has a different history and seems to be entirely the product of the Dark Ages. In legend it is associated with the Arthurian leader Ambrosius and the tyrant Vortigern and it actually contains a pool like the one mentioned in the myth. Thick drystone walls link the craggy outcrops and the fortifications have been dated to the fifth or sixth century. The site was occupied before the Roman period but the defences emerge as a Dark Age reworking of the archaic hillfort concept, presumably undertaken by a local chieftain during the uncertain times which followed the Roman withdrawal. It is also possible that other small Welsh hillforts were built at the same time, as local strongholds against raiders from Ireland.

During the centuries following the Roman withdrawal leadership in English affairs gradually passed into the hands of English-speaking men. There was no great Saxon conquest and British surrender but rather a prolonged and piecemeal emergence of new dynasties. The defenceworks of the period were no longer integrated components of the armour of an empire of conquest stretching from the Middle East to Scotland. Instead they were an incoherent assemblage of decrepit and refurbished strongholds, the modest citadels of local patriarchs and frontier defences constructed in attempts to insulate a province or a locality from the surrounding turmoil.

The frontier defences include a number of impressive examples which, by virtue of the organised toil which they embody, reveal the rise of provincial leaders and warlords who were sufficiently powerful to be able to impose their will upon large workforces. These 'linear earthworks' were not the inventions of the Dark Ages. They are known to have been cast up as territorial boundary markers in Yorkshire and elsewhere during the Bronze Age and more formidable examples were constructed as 'outworks' guarding the approaches to some of the lowland capitals or *oppida* of late Iron Age times. The Antonine wall in Scotland was a much more sophisticated Roman expression of the concept. But earthworks are difficult to date by archaelogical techniques since they pass across open country and any excavated section may not reveal datable evidence of settlement overrun by or developed upon the banks and ditches. Wansdyke in Wessex consists of two linear earthworks or 'dykes' linked by an open stretch of Roman road. East Wansdyke, traversing the chalk country of the Vale of Pewsey, is thought to belong to the fifth or sixth centuries and might be a British-built barrier against the Saxon penetration of Wiltshire from the Thames Valley or, alternatively, a frontierwork of the emerging Saxon kingdom of Wessex. West Wansdyke continues the barrier to a terminus to the south of Bath and might be roughly contemporary with the eastern component.

The Cambridgeshire Dykes are four in number, all straddling the ancient thoroughfare Icknield Way and barring the approaches to East Anglia. They date from some time between the late Roman and middle Saxon periods but because they cannot be closely dated it is not clear whether they were built by Romans to resist barbarian attack, by Saxon settlers to counter British advances from the west, or as frontier defences between Saxon kingdoms. Devil's Dyke is still extremely impressive, its most familiar section dividing the racecourse at Newmarket. It runs south-eastwards for $7\frac{1}{2}$ miles (12km) from the village of Reach where it was linked to a Roman canal which extended the barrier to free movement. With the help of former students, I calculated that this earthwork alone embodied more than 1,800,000 man hours of toil – sufficient to occupy 500 labourers for 400 days. Plainly a great deal of labour was invested in these and the many similar dykes. However, as static defences their value was limited: armies were far too small to allow earthworks like Devil's Dyke to be manned along their length and the military wisdom of extending a force along the crest of a sinuous dyke is debatable. They probably existed as distinctive boundary markers and would also have constituted credible defences against attack by forces of cavalry, any charge foundering in the fronting ditch where riders and mounts could be impaled by missiles hurled down from the bank. In addition, rustlers escaping with stock and booty would have been delayed as they negotiated the ditch and bank, the latter often crowned by a palisade.

The Dark Age frontier work of which we know most is Offa's Dyke, undoubtedly built by Offa, the Mercian king (757–96), to mark the boundary between his realm and the Welsh principalities to the west. The line followed by the dyke is generally sound according to military principles but there is the possibility that it was achieved by negotiation with the Welsh. In any event its very existence proclaimed the might of the Mercian king and left no room for speculation about his resolve to preserve the integrity of his realm. One should never underestimate either the psychological effects of defenceworks or their role as status symbols which underline the power of their creators.

As the political geography of Britain evolved, new territories emerged from the wreckage of empire – youthful and often ephemeral kingdoms which expressed the rise of tribal or national groupings and the successes of ambitious dynasties. The capitals and chief places of these territories are known and one might wonder whether any boasted the turreted trappings of a Camelot? In fact examinations of the archaeological evidence dispel the more glamorous images. Dunadd in Argyll was regarded by most historians as the capital of the seventh- and eighth-century kingdom of Dalriada, established by Scots from Ireland on the western coast of Scotland. Professor Alcock, however, prefers to regard the hill as a special site for the inauguration of Scottish kings. The summit was occupied by a 'nuclear fort', reminiscent of a small prehistoric hillfort, with enclosures looping out towards the lower slopes.

The indigenous people of Dark Age Scotland were Picts, who remain an enigmatic and mysterious nation despite representations of their 'knights' and warriors on their carved symbol stones. Primitive Pictish strongholds appear to be overlain by the medieval castles at Dunottar, near Stonehaven, and Urquhart, in the Great Glen. However, the main Pictish stronghold was at Burghead by the Moray Firth, where the approach to the natural promontory was guarded by three sets of massive ramparts, each about half a mile in length. In 683 Pictish forces laid siege to the Scottish strongholds at Dunadd and Dundurn in Strathearn. Dundurn was another nuclear fort. A palisade of oak staves was superseded by a rubble wall reinforced by nailed oak beams and wickerwork of hazel. When these defences were burned, perhaps by the Picts, the nuclear fort was established with rubble walls up to 25 feet (8m) thick, extending from the citadel to enclose the lower terraces.

In the south of Scotland a British culture endured. Dumbarton has been regarded as the capital of the British territory of Strathclyde with the volcanic outcrop of Castle Rock or *Alt Clut* in Dumbarton harbour providing an admirable citadel. Excavation on the rock revealed a timber and stone look-out platform which was probably burned by Viking raiders from Dublin in 871. More impressive defences here may have been obliterated during the building of medieval or seventeenth-century defences. Anglo-Saxon settlers advanced towards Scotland from the south-east and a fortress town of Colodaesburg within which the monastery of St Aebbe's grew up was established. A possible site for this fortress was discovered by Professor Alcock at Kirk Hill near St Abb's. Here a double palisade of oak beams infilled by wickerwork was later overlain by a 10 foot (3m) high turf rampart to which stone revetments were added. The palisade could have been the defences of Colodaesburg and the turf wall possibly the vallum of the monastery.

Bamburgh in Northumberland was the capital of the English kingdom of Northumbria, where the rocky outcrop supporting the spectacular medieval castle provided a defensive nucleus. Bede (c. 673–735) described Bamburgh as a walled city and related how King Penda of Mercia attempted to destroy it by lighting bonfires around its wall. Little is known about the defences of Dark Age Bamburgh. Founded by Ida of Northumbria in 547, the site was later superseded by a rampart.

In reality Bamburgh was not a glittering metropolis and probably amounted to little more than an enclosed village of timber dwellings. While Burghead, located in the least 'civilised' corner of Britain, was a massive stronghold the other chief places of Arthurian times and those which followed were scarcely majestic. Contemporary writers such as Bede may have thought that they were, or have heard that they were, but what seemed like a city to them would appear as a shabby little shanty town to our eyes.

The perpetuation of outmoded strongholds such as duns, the reworking of archaic concepts of military engineering which produced new hillforts, nuclear forts and linear earthworks, and the reoccupation of derelict hillforts made up the fixed defences of the Dark Ages. While Hollywood has dealt in images of knights in burnished armour and the towering battlements of magnificent kingship, the reality of the times involved small, highly mobile armies scarcely more numerous or sophisticated than bands of brigands; primitive strongpoints which were little more than garrison posts, and insecure kings who progressed from one guard post to the next on a perpetual circuit, knowing that the fall of a strategic little garrison could expose the entire realm to invasion and annexation.

The progress from chaos, through the emergence of provincial kingdoms, towards unification was slow and painful. Sufficient stability was achieved to allow monastic churches to appear and flourish but any dawning of a new age of promise ended abruptly with the eruption of Viking raids. In 787 three shiploads of armed strangers struck in Wessex and in 793 the monastery on Lindisfarne was ravaged by the Vikings; a new age of darkness followed. While ancient hillforts occasionally featured in the conflicts, the wars gave birth to two main types of military monuments: the defended camp and the fortress town. In a few cases the camps provided nuclei for urban growth while in numerous instances the planned fortified settlements or *burhs*, founded by Alfred and his successors, lived on as towns or villages.

The Viking invasions provided a challenge to the Saxon kings of England which at first seemed insurmountable. The raids and advances were unpredictable and it was difficult for poorly financed and unstable governments to support standing armies on revenues derived from an essentially peasant economy. Even when such defence forces could be assembled it was difficult to deploy them, since nobody could know where the next blow would fall. In the course of the ninth century the raids grew in intensity and the Viking presence in parts of England became more sustained as armies of invaders wintered in fortified camps. Some of these camps remain to be discovered and others are debatable – Clare Camp, in Suffolk, is an example. A double rampart and ditch surround a rectangular enclosure of 6.4 acres (2.6ha) overlooking a tributary of the River Stour; this might be an Iron Age hillfort or a Viking stronghold. Several military camps of the invaders were developed and expanded to become fortified Danish towns. These include Derby, Leicester, Lincoln, Stamford, Northampton, Cambridge, Huntingdon and Nottingham, where the lay-out of the Danish settlement was preserved in the street pattern in the south-eastern quarter of the medieval town. Some of these foundations were established around or beside the decayed remnants of Roman civilisation, as at Lincoln and Cambridge, but the most interesting example is that of Stamford. The town embodies not one but two Dark Age fortresses, a Danish one on the north side of the River Welland dating from around 877 and an English one just to the south of the river crossing, created after 918 when Edward the Elder captured Viking Stamford.

A great deal remains to be learned about the location and lay-out of Viking winter camps. One lying to the north of the Saxon church at Repton in Derbyshire has been explored. It is associated with a scene of ghastly carnage, for a sunken Saxon chapel here was used as a mass mausoleum to contain 159 completely dismembered bodies, perhaps those of soldiers of the Mercian army defeated in 873.

At the start of 878 Guthrum's Danish army violated the conventional Christmas truce and invaded Wessex. For some months King Alfred was obliged to lead the life of a hunted guerrilla fighter but then emerged to inflict a series of defeats on the Danes, culminating in the battle of Edington, in Wiltshire. The King sought to consolidate his victory by establishing a system of strongholds or *burhs*. Previously these were regarded as fortresses, but more recent interpretations view them as fortified towns. It is clear that the *burhs* were a varied collection, both in terms of their original lay-out and their later success. Some at least were planned settlements surrounded by earthen defenceworks, the inspiration for these carefully planned forms presumably being derived from the ruined or semi-derelict Roman towns. Winchester was almost certainly one of Alfred's foundation. Here the entire 144 acres (58ha) protected by the defences appears to have been set out with a regular gridwork of streets producing 5.4 miles (8.63km) of surfaced road. These streets divided the town into a series of rectangular property blocks. Initially each block may have accommodated the dwelling of its owner and his church, with a later sub-division of blocks between adjacent properties. By the middle of the tenth century the High Street was probably packed with dwellings and shops and by the end of this century traders had become concentrated in particular streets, like Shieldwright Street and Tanner Street. At Cricklade, in contrast, extensive areas inside the defences remained underdeveloped.

If the internal lay-out of some *burhs* was influenced by Roman town planning, the defensive concept was probably inspired by experience gained in fighting the Danes. As yet very little is known about the Danish camps, but it is clear that they were created as temporary army bases. They enabled the invaders to avoid fighting pitched battles against the English, for when threatened the Danes would retire within the protection of their earthen ramparts, emerging again to pillage when the threat was lifted. In copying and redeveloping the concept of the fortress camp Alfred produced a form of town unique in Europe. The *burhs* were established on a grand scale, it being Alfred's intention that no part of his Wessex kingdom should be more than 20 miles (32km) from such a stronghold.

The defences of the *burhs* consisted of earth or turf ramparts which presented a steep face to the attacker, with one or more deep ditches in front of the rampart. Sections of such ramparts, often much eroded, can be seen at towns like Cricklade, Wallingford and Wareham. Around the inside of the rampart ran a street which allowed the rapid deployment of defending forces. It was probably intended from the outset that the *burhs* should develop their own economic life and a law of Alfred's successor, Edward the Elder, decreed that 'no one shall buy or sell except in a market town with the witness of the port-reeve and of other men of credit'. It is likely that tradesmen were attracted to the *burhs* by tax incentives and low rents – the same sort of inducements offered by the new towns of the twentieth century.

Edward the Elder continued the establishment of *burhs*, some of his foundations being 'double *burhs*' composed of fortified settlements on both sides of a river crossing. Nottingham is an example. In Mercia Queen Aethelflaed also introduced *burhs*, as at Warwick, Stafford and at Worcester, where the *burh* was decreed to be built for the protection of all people and markets were established in the market place, in the streets and outside the fortifications. Hereford may originally have been fortified by King Offa to resist Welsh invasion but was redeveloped as a *burh* in the tenth century.

Around AD 919 a document known as the Burghal Hidage was compiled which listed the existing *burhs*. It reveals a diverse collection of centres. Some, like Wareham and Wallingford, were fortress towns of the type described. Some were Roman centres where the old fortifications were re-used, as at Portchester, and Chichester, Towcester and Winchester were among several redeveloped Roman settlements. Many, like Hastings and Oxford, prospered, though others, like Langport in Somerset, sank into the village ranks. A few, like Lyng in Somerset, were virtually stillborn or existed as little more than an ancient hillfort, like Chisbury Camp in Wiltshire.

One of the lost *burh* sites was discovered recently when *Cledemutha* was recognised as having lain near the mouth of the River Clwyd near Rhuddlan in North Wales. The *burh* was established by Edward the Elder in 921 to defend the coast against incursions by Vikings. An area of about 75 acres (30ha) was en-

closed by earthbanks to complete a chain of forts which extended
via Chester to Manchester. A great ditch some 50 feet (15m) wide
and ten feet (3m) deep was dug, with the upcast being used to build
an inner bank or rampart of slippery clay. Within these substantial
and extensive defences Edward must have intended to establish a
town of English settlers but Welsh revolts later in the century will
have prevented the establishment of a settled population. Subsequently, the site was secured by a Norman motte and a town was
established in its shadow; by 1086 it had eighteen burgesses and a
church. A third town at Rhuddlan was founded by Edward I in 1278
beside the imposing stone castle, one of several built to secure his
grip on north Wales.

The introduction of the *burhs* marked a return to the concept of
the communal stronghold, as previously epitomised by the hillfort,
and to the Roman notion of an integrated system of defences –
though in Saxon times it was the kingdom rather than the empire
which was being protected against outsiders. The *burh* strategy was
important and successful; it was the main prong in a defence policy
which also entailed the creation of a navy and the bribing of
the aggressor with payments of Danegeld. However, it was not
paralleled by the establishment of anything comparable to the
castles of the medieval period. Had Saxon castles existed they
would doubtless now be buried and overgrown ruins. Instead the
age provided us with Winchester, Lewes, Oxford, Malmesbury,
Nottingham and a wealth of other towns – no mean legacy even
though their origins are largely forgotten.

The paucity of castles in England must have made it easier for the
Norman invaders to establish their ascendancy after their victory at
Hastings. Writing around 1125 Ordericus Vitalis explained that:

> . . . The fortresses which the Gauls call castles had been very
> few in the English provinces, and for this reason the English,
> although warlike and courageous, had nevertheless shown
> themselves too weak to withstand their enemies.

Chapter Four

The shell keep at Restormel.

THE COMING OF THE CASTLE

There were castles in England at the time of the Norman conquest, but these were mainly Norman castles, few in number and built by favourites of Edward the Confessor (1042–66). Within a few decades of the Conquest, however, castles were numerous, the symbols of defeat and humiliation.

Saxon society had been rigidly stratified and war was no stranger to the countryside, so one would expect that castles would have evolved. However it appears that only rather modest private strongholds materialised in the forms of towers and circular enclosures or 'ringworks'. Documentary evidence of Saxon castles scarcely exists apart from one mention dating from a little before the Conquest which explains how a man seeking to gain access to the ranks of the nobility should acquire, amongst other things, a chapel, a bell house, a kitchen and a 'castle gate'. It is not clear whether this last named building was some form of gatehouse, a watch tower or something equivalent to the pele houses of much later centuries. But it is safe to assume that if such strongholds were substantial, formidable and numerous then archaeology would have explored several examples.

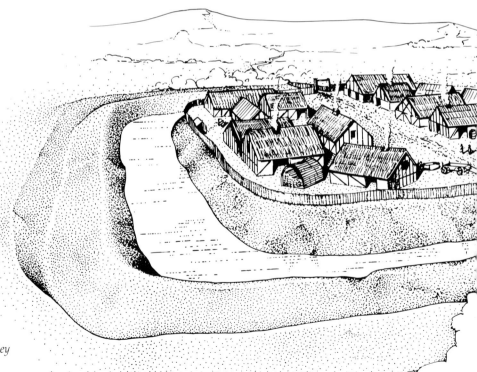

A reconstruction of a Norman motte and bailey castle.

During the Saxon period stone was almost exclusively reserved for church building and many timber-framed churches were rebuilt in stone during the Saxon era. In some cases these churches had disproportionately large towers, and, since towers were of secondary importance so far as the ritual of worship was concerned and were omitted from many Saxon and Norman designs, it is reasonable to suppose that some of these towers were provided, at least in part, as bolt-holes. A great many of our parish churches began as the private chapels of estate-owning families and the proprietorial interest could have been perpetuated in the church which doubled as a family stronghold. Probably the best example is at Earls Barton in Northamptonshire. The original nave of the church occupied the base of the massive tower and the building stands on a spur which is guarded by apparently prehistoric earthworks.

In the same county the base of a Saxon tower embedded in the earthworks of a Norman 'ringwork' has been excavated at Sulgrave. Ringworks are defenceworks composed of a circular earthbank or rampart surrounded by a deep ditch. They are known to have been constructed in Britain during the same period that

The timber keep tower, which would have had the lord's hall at the middle level, his private apartment above and a storeroom below.

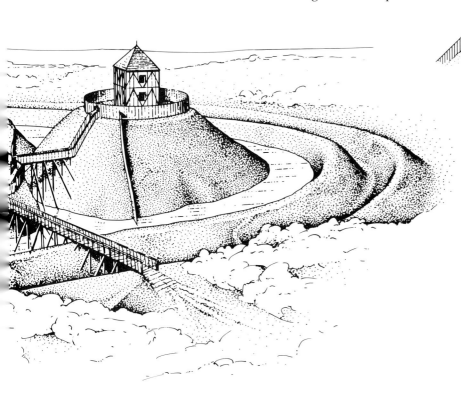

mottes and motte-and-bailey castles were erected, but recent evidence suggests that some ringworks in England predated the Norman conquest. One excavated at Goltho in Lincolnshire definitely seems to date from around AD 1000. In Ireland small ringworks, known as 'raths', are remarkably common and more than 35,000 examples are known. The vast majority existed as fortified farmsteads, the abodes of the leading lights in local rural society, and the range of dates obtained from rath excavations is quite amazing, some raths being prehistoric creations and others belonging to the medieval period.

Experimentation with earthen defenceworks in Britain began in Neolithic times and reached its pinnacle of achievement in the great hillforts of the Iron Age. These great fortresses were communal strongholds, while those of the Norman period were private castles built, by and large, to pacify and even oppress rather than to protect the surrounding population. Despite the long established tradition of earthen defences the motte was not an indigenous development but a military import from the Continent. A motte was an artificial hill of a flat-topped conical form which was normally surrounded by a ditch or moat from which the motte-building materials were excavated. The word 'motte' relates to turf and the motte was turfed or made of sods. Most of the more substantial mottes had a bailey attached, a roughly oval enclosure guarded by an earthen rampart.

The first castles recorded in England, and described by the word 'castel', are mentioned fifteen years before the Norman conquest. Three castle owners are named and two more castles are implied. Clavering in Essex has been suggested as the location of one of these mottes but the remainder may have been in Herefordshire. The most securely identified of these pre-Norman mottes is at Ewas Harold, where the substantial motte occupies a sloping ridge and overlooks its bailey. It has been linked to the 'Pentecost's Castle' of the old documents and was refortified by William fitzOsbern shortly after the Conquest. The small handful of mottes existing before 1066 were built by Norman favourites and supporters of Edward the Confessor. There is also the possibility that Edward's successor, Harold Godwinson, established a castle inside the prehistoric fortification at Dover.

The castle was almost as new to Normandy as it was to England. Mentions of castles of this type in France appear after 1020 and the word 'dungio' was applied to a castle built by the Scheldt near Cambrai in 979. The evolution of the motte is still debated. Dr Brian

Hope-Taylor has described how the motte could have developed from Roman watch towers which were raised on stilts to overlook the German frontier of the empire. By heaping earth around the timber legs of such towers the progression towards the motte might have been set in motion. Another, rather more convincing, argument derives the motte from the ringwork, for by heightening the ramparts and infilling the centre of a small ringwork a motte would result.

Mottes, baileys and defensive towers or 'keeps', though quite different in appearance, could be found in combination – the keep could be freestanding or it might crown a motte or be encircled by a bailey. Meanwhile, ringworks provided an alternative to mottes and could also protect a keep. All these defences were characteristic of a feudal society, for they guarded the abode or base of a feudal magnate – they were private fortifications. The lord might be afraid of his tenants, his neighbours or his king, or all of them at once. If he decided to fortify his home, the result was a keep. If he defended its immediate approaches then a motte was created, while if he chose

The Norman motte at Berkhamsted.

to guard the ground within which it stood then a bailey resulted. Having said this, many of the smaller keeps and mottes were bolt-holes occupied only when the threats materialised and the house and its outbuildings might stand in the protective shadow of these strongholds, within the bailey.

The Norman repertoire of castles was imported by the invaders. As the conquering army dispersed one can imagine the Continental lords, mercenaries and carpetbaggers exploring their new estates. The lands that they had won were held by force of arms. Most of the English lords had been dispossessed and revolts, large and small, rippled across the countryside. As he entered his new estates the foreign lord would cast about for a defensible site which he could fortify, and he would need to choose which type of stronghold to build. If there was a suitable rocky outcrop it would probably be exploited. Thin topsoil and exposed rock discouraged the building of earthen defences but the steep rock faces could easily be quarried for stone. In such circumstances a stone keep was favoured. Examples of such castles were built from the outset; the surviving keep at Peveril Castle in Derbyshire dates from 1175 but its predecessor, overlooking a steep limestone gorge on the outskirts of Castleton, seems also to have been of stone. The keep of the Tower of London, the White Tower, was begun about a decade after the Conquest. Many estates lacked natural bastions and artificial landscaping was applied to enhance the defences of hills, slopes or ridges or to create a stronghold on a site which had no obvious attractions. In a few cases, like Saltwood in Kent, water defences were created by damming a valley, while the castles at Knepp in Sussex and Skipsea in Yorkshire were raised in marshes. At Skipsea the motte was raised in a mere, the eel-rich waters of which separated it from the earthworks of its bailey. Its first owner Drogo de Bevrere, however, spent little time appreciating his defences. Twenty years after the Conquest he murdered his wife, an ill-judged move, not least because she was related to the Conqueror. He then dashed away to meet William before news of the deed could reach him and borrowed money from the king on the pretext that he needed it to take his wife to Flanders, spending it to make his own escape to the Continent.

In several cases use was made of pre-existing fortifications. The most impressive example is at Portchester in Hampshire, where the Norman keep of around 1120 was built in the north-west corner of the rectangular walled enclosure of the Roman Saxon shore fort. At

Tomen-y-Mur on the moors inland from Harlech the motte occupied and partly obliterated the ramparts of a Roman garrison post, and Brough Castle in Cumbria was built inside the earthworks of a Roman auxiliary fort. The Norman motte-and-bailey castle at Barwick-in-Elmet in Yorkshire occupies a corner of an Iron Age hillfort and in Gwynedd an ancient round barrow was adopted as the base of a motte.

The scale of defences reflected both the resources of the owners and the nature of the threat. Mottes could be gigantic mounds, like the ones at Norwich and Thetford, or relative molehills less than the height of a man. Evidence both from contemporary accounts and from archaeological work shows that the flat summits of the mounds were usually encircled by a palisade of stakes, while timber keeps or watch towers were erected within the palisade on all but the smallest mottes. Around 1130 an ecclesiastical biographer wrote of the country to the south-east of Calais:

> It is the custom . . . to make a mound of earth as high as they can and then dig about it as wide and deep as possible. The space on top of the mound is enclosed by a palisade of very strong hewn logs, strengthened at intervals by as many towers as their means can provide. Inside the enclosure is a citadel, or keep, which commands the whole circuit of the defences.

Excavations at Abinger motte in Surrey in 1949–50, and more recently at Keir Knowe of Drum, near Stirling, uncovered the post holes of both the palisade and the keep.

Such castles were not as primitive as one might imagine. Attackers, particularly if they were armoured, would have had great difficulty in scaling the steep slopes of a motte – and it has been suggested that the slopes of these mounds were sometimes coated in slippery clay. In several cases timber defences were superseded by walls of stone, which had the advantage of fire resistance. Quite sophisticated military architecture could be accomplished in timber and there is an eleventh-century record of a timber keep of three storeys being built in Northern France. Not all timber fortifications were shortlived; recent excavations at the motte-and-bailey castle at Hen Domen, Montgomery, have shown that this frontier fort, built before 1086, was not superseded by the stone walls of Montgomery castle until 1223 and even then it served the castle as an advance look-out post until 1300.

The proliferation of castles was a deliberate facet of Norman policy (a prefabricated timber fort was brought across the Channel with William's invasion). The Anglo-Saxon Chronicle describes the policy tersely: 'Castles he caused to be made, and poor men to be greatly oppressed.' Cambridge, Huntingdon, Lincoln, Nottingham, Warwick and York were all fortified, sometimes at the expense of their unfortunate inhabitants. At Norwich 113 houses were demolished to make way for the castle mound with its 380 feet (116m) summit diameter and at Lincoln 166 households were rendered homeless by the castle works. In addition to the castles created by the king and garrisoned by his lieutenants, a host of lesser castles were initiated by the provincial and local lords. From the English the Normans inherited problems of guarding the Welsh border while Anglo-Norman settlers, mainly the allies of the Scottish monarchy, built large numbers of mottes in Southern Scotland during the twelfth century. By 1970 some 239 Scottish mottes had been identified, some of them standing upon older ringworks. Freestanding keeps of timber or stone were sometimes built and ringworks were constructed in great numbers. Nevertheless they were outnumbered by mottes in a ratio of three or four to one.

Most mottes were associated with baileys. Some had only one attached bailey, though others had as many as five. Where several existed, the more valuable assets would be kept in the more strongly defended of the enclosures. Lewes Castle was most unusual in having two mottes at either end of a single bailey. The bailey was not an empty compound but contained a range of useful outbuildings and often the main dwelling of the owner. At Hen Domen the motte stood at the western end of an oval bailey which was guarded by an outer bank and two ramparts. Excavation of about half the area of the bailey has revealed over fifty timber structures belonging to five major phases of occupation. They range from small sheds to impressive halls and include granaries, chapels, towers and storerooms. During the first phase of the castle, beginning around 1070, a massive two-storey timber hall was built and was entered at ground-floor level, the visitor ascending a staircase to its upper storey and exiting via a door at first-floor level.

Normally the motte was placed on the perimeter of the main bailey, though there were exceptions, like Barwick-in-Elmet, where it stands at the centre of massive bailey earthworks. Baileys could also be attached to ringworks, as at Castle Rising in Norfolk. Since the motte normally functioned as the ultimate element in a sequence of defences of increasing strength, it needed to be separated from the main bailey by a deep ditch. This ditch was bridged to allow day-to-day movement between the motte and the bailey but the bridge had to be raised or broken when defenders retreated from the bailey to the motte. The Bayeux Tapestry depicts the mottes at Dol, Rennes, Dinan and Bayeux in Normandy, with their timber keeps and palisades, and the motte bridge at Rennes is plainly shown. At Hen Domen a sequence of flying bridges was excavated. In some cases timber bridges were not employed and solid causeways were used, as at Abinger. Such causeways could not be broken by defenders and were less advantageous in military terms. The ramparts of the bailey could be palisaded or hedged in thorns and brambles. At Farnham Castle in Surrey the bailey was defended by a dead hedge of cut thorns and the renewal of the hedge continued into the thirteenth century.

Castles of timber fitted the needs of newly installed lords who faced the possibility of insurgency at any moment. Stone castles took longer to build and were more costly, especially if the stone had to be quarried elsewhere and brought to the site by barges or carts. A few castles had masonry features virtually from the beginning, and in addition to the White Tower these included those at Richmond in Yorkshire, Colchester, Ludlow and Corfe. In the case of the White Tower, William erected a castle to dominate London immediately after the Conquest. Two sides were provided by an angle of the Roman wall, while to the north and west a ditch, rampart and palisade were employed. At Rochester, too, the Norman castle, begun in 1087, refortified an angle formed by Roman walls. Within a decade the stone keep was begun with the existing defences being retained as a bailey. Throughout much of Southern and Eastern England a shortage of good building stone presented a problem. The White Tower was built of local ragstone rubble with good, shaped stones being reserved for the dressings. Canterbury Castle, built around 1086, had walls of rubble dressed with top-class stone imported across the Channel from Caen, and at Colchester the castle used rubble laced with courses of bricks which were pillaged from the ruins of Roman Colchester. East Anglia was particularly impoverished of good stone, and when the de Veres built their great stone keep at Hedingham in Essex after 1130 its walls were of rubble faced with stone imported from the renowned

The dominating Norman keep at Richmond.

quarries at Barnack near Peterborough, about forty miles from Hedingham and considerably further via the tracks and waterways used in transporting the stone.

Each type of earth or timber defencework had its equivalent in stone. The stone keep was plainly comparable to timber keep towers. When translated into stone, the palisade which ringed the top of a motte produced a 'shell keep', like the one at Castle Acre in Norfolk, while curtain walls enclosing a fortified site performed the same role as the rampart and palisade of the bailey. Most typically the early stone castle consisted of a tower or else a shell keep and a single fortified ward with a relatively low curtain wall. At Richmond, built after 1071, the plan was unusual. The steep slope overlooking the River Swale was probably defended by a timber palisade and the triangular bailey was created by building two massive curtain walls to the north of it with a two-storey rectangular gate tower at their convergence. A tower was built in the south-west angle and three towers punctuated the north-east wall. The keep, surviving virtually intact, was added about a century later and swallowed up the original gate tower.

Where the keep was built on a pre-existing motte the builders had to be confident that the soil had become sufficiently compacted to bear the weight of all the masonry. In some cases, however, the tower was built on solid foundations and then earth was heaped around the tower base, creating the illusion that the motte was supporting the tower. At Lydford in Devon, for example, excavation of the low motte revealed window slits near the base of the tower which had been obscured when the mound had been raised around the keep. In other cases, like Winchester, keep foundations were sunk down deeply into an existing motte, while in others still the foundations were only shallow. Longtown Castle in Hereford-shire was built as a squat, circular keep on an older rectangular mound of unknown origins and the shallow foundations have proved inadequate. When a buttressed four-storey rectangular keep was added to the oval motte at Clun in Shropshire around 1150 the builders clearly had doubts about the land-bearing capacity of the earthwork. They built the tower in a peculiar position against the sloping side of the motte, with one wall in the ditch and the facing wall on top of the motte. Thus from the crown of the motte one could actually look down into the two lower storeys of the tower. A similar position was chosen for the rec-tangular keep at Guildford in Surrey. At Farnham the mound, which was built around 1140, supported a square stone keep and contained a substantial stone well chamber. The keep was con-fiscated and dismantled by Henry II in 1155 and replaced with a new castle when the de Blois family regained their estates. The bottom rim of the motte was cut back and a circular wall some 40 feet (12m) high was built around it. The space between the wall and the old motte was then filled with earth to produce a drum-shaped structure of earth and rubble revetted in stone and a circular shell keep was built on top of this drum.

Freestanding stone keeps were obviously considered to be

sufficiently strong to resist attack without the assistance of the steep upward approaches endowed by mottes. The walls of the White Tower were some 12 to 15 feet (3.5 to 4.5m) in thickness, those at Canterbury were more than 9 feet (c. 3m) thick and those at Chepstow almost 9 feet (c. 3m) thick. The majority of the greater Norman stone keeps were freestanding and relied on the armour of their masonry and the outer defences of the bailey. Characteristically their walls were strengthened by broad, shallow buttresses, while the vulnerable entrances were placed at second-storey level and were reached via external stone stairways. At Newcastle and Dover, however, the builders went one better and placed the entrances at third-floor level. The entrance usually gave access to the great hall, which was the social, domestic and administrative hub of the castle and its territory. Wall chambers opened off from the hall and a mural gallery often ran around its walls at a high level. The floor level below the great hall was normally devoted to storage and would house the garrison in the event of war. The floor above provided domestic accommodation and beds could have been placed in alcoves. This would also be the very last resort of defenders, though once the lower levels of the keep had been taken then really its fate was sealed. To see the interior of a keep preserved in all its austere Norman dignity one can do no better than visit Hedingham Castle. In the White Tower the entrance gave access to the hall at second-storey level, while the chapel on the third storey was later subdivided by the insertion of a new floor to create a fourth storey. The keep at Colchester Castle covered a greater area of ground but its third storey is missing and may never have been completed.

The weakness of the stone keep lay in its vulnerability to determined attacks on the wall base and to sapping to undermine a corner angle of the tower. At Hedingham the walls are 10 to 12 feet (3 to 3.5m) thick and they splay outwards at ground-floor level to produce an even broader platform. Canterbury, Newcastle and Scarborough are among the various other Norman castles to display this feature. At Conisbrough in Yorkshire, one of the first of a new generation of circular keeps was built around 1180. The cylindrical tower was strengthened by six great buttresses and the plinth is massive and splayed. The whole structure – apart from the uppermost tier of battlements – survives as a monument to the paranoia of the keep-owning classes.

The stone keep tower was not a particularly innovative form of

The keep of Appleby Castle.

stronghold. The keeps contained little that would have seemed new to Roman eyes and their construction embodied less skill than did that of a typical broch. Their security derived from the sheer weight of the masonry rather than from any particular sophistication. Several enjoyed good fortune which, coupled with the strength of their walls, has allowed them to survive virtually intact to the present day. These survivors are still impressive but in their day, when only a handful of cathedrals could exceed their stone-built majesty, they were immeasurably more imposing. Dover, Rochester, Portchester, Hedingham, Richmond, Ludlow and the White Tower are all sure to fire the imagination of the visitor and partly ruined keeps, like the ones at Scarborough, or Corfe in Dorset, can still impress. Though left far behind by developments in military engineering, some square keeps were still considered worthy of refortification long after their original construction. At Appleby in Cumbria the keep was built on an old motte-and-bailey site around 1180 as a cube-shaped structure measuring 50 feet (15m) in all three dimensions. At the end of the following century its height was increased by about a third by the addition of a new upper storey which might have been intended to serve as a final refuge should the Scottish invaders have succeeded in penetrating the base of the tower.

Both Appleby and Dover keeps were originally built to a somewhat squat, cube-shaped plan and the quest for breadth and solidity rather than height produced a special class of keeps known as 'hall keeps'. A superb example survives at Castle Rising in Norfolk, along with the well-preserved earthworks of a large Norman ringwork with baileys to east and west. The keep standing within the ringwork was built of only two storeys and rises to a height of about 50 feet (15m) but the broad groundplan allowed for a more spacious interior lay-out and both storeys were divided by an internal wall. On the upper storey division and subdivision allowed a great hall, kitchen, great chamber, chapel and ante-chapel to be accommodated. The keep was built around 1140 and was strongly protected by outer defences. From the top of the ringwork there was a fall of some 30 feet (9m) to the bottom of the encircling ditch and the crest was crowned by a curtain wall which is thought to have been strengthened by three wall towers. This wall has gone although portions of the gatehouse still survive.

Middleham Castle in Yorkshire is a good but less complete example of a hall keep. In 1086 a serviceable motte-and-bailey castle was built on a hill about a quarter of a mile to the south-west of the later castle. A century later Robert fitzRalph opted to build a more prestigious stronghold but selected a much poorer site which was overlooked by higher ground. Relying on the strength of massive walls, he created a great squat keep 55 feet (17m) in height by some 105 feet (32m) by 78 feet (24m) in plan. As at Castle Rising, an interior wall subdivided the spacious interior. The lofty and imposing

*The well-preserved keep at
Hedingham.*

The hall keep at Castle Rising.

tower keep at Scarborough had four storeys and it provided its occupants with a total floor space of 3500 square feet ($325m^2$), while Middleham boasted one of 9000 square feet ($841m^2$) – an indication of the domestic advantages of the hall keep design. With its capacious interior the hall keep dispensed with any need to provide a separate hall for residential and communal use. In comparison, at Richmond the keep was purely a military building and the lord had his residential suite in the adjacent Scolland's Hall. Any defences which may have guarded the vicinity of fitzRalph's castle were obliterated by the expansion of the townlet of Middleham and by the building of subsequent fortifications. In the thirteenth century the keep was hemmed in by a curtain wall which seems to have underlined the status of the 'mansion' rather than to have added greatly to its strength, while the development of offices, apartments, a mill, bakehouse and brewhouse buildings along the curtain in the two following centuries must have cramped the confines of the castle. A fine three-storey gatehouse was added in the fourteenth century.

Norham in Northumberland was a late expression of the hall keep concept, built after 1157 on the site of a ringwork-and-bailey castle twice captured by Scottish invaders earlier in the century. This was a three-storey keep and the division between tower keeps and hall keeps is not clear-cut; the White Tower could be regarded as an early but far from primitive hall keep.

A few stone keeps, like the White Tower and Colchester, were built when the Norman Conquest was still a fresh memory. A few more, like Lydney in Gloucestershire and Ascot D'Oyly in Oxfordshire, were built during the troubled reign of Stephen (1135–54), when magnates looked to their own defences and un-licensed or 'adulterine' castles proliferated. Most stone keeps were a product of the reign of Henry II (1154–89), a strong and purpose-ful king who destroyed some illegal castles of the preceding reign, erected great royal keeps to secure his kingdom and occasionally allowed trusted members of his nobility to built their own strong-holds. In 1174 Bishop Hugh Purset's castle at Norham was surren-dered to the king because this Bishop of Durham's loyalty was deemed suspect.

Stone tower keeps are probably the most potent symbols of Norman domination. Sometimes, as in the case of the one at Richmond, they still seem to glower masterfully across the sur-rounding territory. However, alternative forms of stone castle existed and were often preferred. Although examples of early stone keeps have been given, initially the shell keep seems to have been a more popular design. Several display masonry laid in the herring-bone fashion with courses of slanting stones. This form of building is thought to belong to the years before 1100 and can also be seen in the inner walling of the early tower keep at Colchester.

Shell keeps standing on mounds enjoyed the advantages which these steepsided earthworks provided. However, their position on top of such artificial hills could give rise to problems of unstable foundations, so that their walls were seldom built very high. The lord might have his timber domestic and service buildings sited in a bailey below, but often they would have been placed around the inner face of the shell wall, looking inwards to a central courtyard. Most shell keeps stood on mottes, though this was not invariably the case. The most impressive exception to this rule is Restormel

Castle in Cornwall. A castle was begun here by Baldwin fitzTurstin around 1100 to dominate a crossing on the River Fowey. The walls of the shell keep stand on the natural ground level and the illusion of a low motte was created by the heaping of earth around the base of these walls. The castle stands within the broad ditch of a ringwork. Late in the thirteenth century a rectangular tower was added as a projection from the north-east side of the curtain wall and two-storey buildings were constructed within the walls to surround the central courtyard. Stores and accommodation for the garrison were provided at ground-floor level while halls, private apartments and a kitchen existed above.

Elsewhere in Cornwall a very fine shell keep which is completely different in appearance can be admired at Launceston. The castle stands on a steep motte and looks for all the world like a gigantic bell-push. This was the place selected by the Conqueror's brother, Robert de Mortain, as the hub of his newly-gained Cornish estates. On taking possession of his lands after the Conquest he sculpted the motte and crowned it with a castle of unknown form which endured until the early thirteenth century. It was then replaced with a massively built shell keep with walls which were 12 feet (3.7m) thick and which rose to a height of more than 30 feet (9m). The bailey below was enclosed by a wall and originally part of this curtain shielded the steps which ascended the motte. Rather later in the century, around 1240, Richard, Earl of Cornwall, the brother of Henry III, removed the buildings which nestled inside the shell keep and replaced them with a cylindrical tower. Its base occupied almost half the diameter of the keep and it rose to twice the height of the encircling walls. The gap between the new tower and the shell keep was roofed over and a parapet was added to create a fighting platform. With the provision of a new battlemented wall around the base of the old shell defenders could now be arranged in three tiers, the top tier occupying the top of the tower.

Henry II improved several royal castles by building shell keeps upon their mottes. The list includes Hastings, Arundel in Sussex, Tickhill in Yorkshire and the Round Tower at Windsor. William the Conqueror had established a motte-and-bailey castle at Windsor very shortly after the Conquest. The motte was created by improving a natural chalk hillock and upon it he built an imposing shell keep of local sandstone and surrounded the bailey with a curtain wall. Henry's castle was a new shell keep erected directly inside the walls of the Conqueror's castle, with the original walls

left standing and supporting a terraced walkway around the new keep. During rebuilding under George IV (1820–30) Henry's tower was raised and converted into a great stone cylinder which stands twice as high as the medieval castle.

The unusual shell keep at Launceston.

Other notable shell keeps include those at Pickering, Tonbridge, Lewes, Carisbrooke on the Isle of Wight, Berkhamsted, Warwick, Lincoln, Totnes, Tamworth, Degannwy and Cardiff. Several once-important examples have not survived, such as the former shell keeps at Bedford, Oxford, Southampton, Hereford and Gloucester. Sometimes the sites of ruined shell keeps still exude a certain grandeur by virtue of the associated earthworks – Berkhamsted, the massive motte at Clare in Suffolk and the haunting relics of Castle Acre in Norfolk are all examples. One of the most dramatic scenic pageants is found at Durham, where keep and cathedral stand on a red sandstone bluff embraced on three sides by a tight meander loop of the River Wear. The castle on this fine natural site was begun in 1072 in order to provide previously insecure Norman Bishops of Durham with a powerfully fortified residence within their hostile territory. The bailey was built to a triangular plan, the base of the triangle looking westward over the steep descent to the river and the octagonal shell keep standing in the apex of the triangle, its foundations dug into the rock and its walls of locally hewn stone. Buttresses braced each of the angles apart from the one supported by the bailey wall. The shell keep was described by Laurence of Durham around 1145; he mentions the buttressed walls, suggests that the ground level inside the keep was raised and that the timber buildings within rose high above the encircling walls. Much of what is seen today dates from a comprehensive rebuilding in 1838–40, when the keep was converted to serve the needs of Durham University.

Norman castles of conquest were exported into Wales and were introduced to Scotland mainly by Anglo-Norman supporters of the Scottish monarchy. Rothesay Castle on the Isle of Bute was built around 1150 as a typical shell keep but was unusual in lacking any associated bailey. The walls were built some 9 feet (c. 3m) thick and stood more than 20 feet (6m) high. Unlike some other spectacular castles, it experienced a spectacular history. In 1230 Norsemen exployed a 'cat' or 'sow' device to breach the walls. This was a robust wooden penthouse roofed in wet skins to protect the attackers from missiles and fire as they burrowed with crowbars. The gap which they wrought can still be seen, although most of the surviving masonry dates from the late fourteenth to sixteenth centuries. The castle was a favoured resort of the early Stewart kings and the title 'Duke of Rothesay' has been bestowed upon heirs to the Scottish throne since the reign of Robert III (1390–1406).

Tower keeps and shell keeps existed as formidable bastions of last resort. Unlike the early castle at Rothesay, most were guarded by the outer defences of the bailey or baileys and defenders would hope that assaults could be repulsed at the bailey without their assailants gaining the opportunity to test the strength of the keep masonry. The building of curtain walls represented an upgrading of the rampart palisade defences of the typical early building. Sometimes the military budget was biased in favour of a strong keep, but sometimes the curtain received the bulk of the defence expenditure. As we have seen, at Richmond the curtain wall was the original main component of the Norman castle. On the whole, however, Norman curtain walls tended to be rather modest and unsophisticated compared to the ingenious and cleverly erected arrangements for high vantage points from which defenders could sweep the wall base with missiles that evolved later in the Middle Ages.

At Pickering, a curtain wall was an early feature of the quite complicated evolution of the castle. A timber motte-and-bailey castle may have been established here by William the Conqueror. A stone hall was built within the palisaded defences during the reign of Henry I (1100–1135) and around 1180 the timber palisade of the inner ward was replaced by a curtain wall with a single tower, Coleman Tower, guarding the entrance to the bailey and the access to the motte. About this time the timber keep upon the motte was probably replaced by a stone shell keep, though the remains which survive are those of the new shell keep built during the reign of Henry III (1216–72). Work of a different character was added after the raid into England led by Robert Bruce in 1322. At this time the defences of the outer ward were still of timber but the urgency of the Scottish threat prompted the construction of a strong curtain wall around the outer ward which looped out from the curtain of the inner ward and was studded with three rectangular towers and a gate tower. Now the motte and its keep stood at the centre of a complete ring of walls.

Ludlow is another splendid castle with a complicated evolution. Early in the twelfth century the de Lacy family established a keep-like gate tower here with an entrance passage at ground-floor level and a great hall above. When the passageway was sealed up at each end and converted into a prison the keep took on a more conventional appearance. Around 1180 a curtain wall fronted by a ditch was built to guard the outer bailey and in the thirteenth century round towers were added to the curtain.

Few castles can boast such a long and fascinating history as the one at Dover, where the passing centuries have never devalued the strategic significance of the site as a bastion against invasion. An important hillfort was built here in the Iron Age and the Roman use of the site is still evidenced by the remarkable survival of the *pharos* or lighthouse which they erected above the cliffs. Some form of Saxon stronghold existed there before the Conquest. It was described by William Poitiers as a fortress of great strength and its defences are known to have been strengthened in 1064. This was most probably a *burh* established inside the still imposing ramparts of the old hillfort. The Conqueror also exploited this situation and

The keep at Dover.

erected a timber motte-and-bailey castle on the site. Around 1170 the great stone keep was built, but Henry II was not content to trust in its exceptionally massive walls, built more than 20 feet (6m) thick in places. Instead, the keep served as the hub in an unusually advanced system of defences. Work continued by his son John (1199–1216) resulted in the building of a strong inner curtain wall studded with stone wall towers and a pair of double towered gatehouses and barbicans, and an outer curtain with innovative D-shaped wall towers looping around the northern part of the castle. This outer curtain was extended by Henry III to run southwards to the brow of the cliff.

Another castle with strong curtain walls and a long history of service is Beeston in Cheshire. Returning from a crusade in the

1220s Ranulph, sixth Earl of Chester, fortified a hill commanding ancient routeways to the north-west with inner and outer curtain walls. Only when recent archaeological excavations were begun was it realised that this was also a hillfort site and that the hill had been defended in various ways from the late Bronze Age to the seventeenth century. The medieval builders established their outer curtain wall along the prehistoric rampart which followed the crest of the natural scarp and recut some of the ancient ditches. The modern excavations revealed that roads and trackways of no less than fifteen different ages had approached the outer gateway.

Norman castles do not resemble most storybook castles with turret-studded and battlement-crested walls but they still very strongly evoke the period of conquest and subjugation by foreigners. Study the uncompromising silhouette of Richmond Castle from a distance and it is easy to imagine the province of rebels pinned down by the weight of Norman arms, masonry and ruthlessness. The better preserved the castle the more one is likely to be impressed by the austere dignity of Norman military architecture. Such castles were introduced to Britain in a fairly developed form and did not evolve rapidly, so that some of the most impressive keeps are amongst the earliest. No great ingenuity was expected of the masons, and while many walls were dauntingly thick they consisted of inner and outer skins of shaped stones with the broad space between being packed with rubble. Naturally, almost a thousand years of erosion have roughened the texture of such walls, especially where softer sandstones and mediocre limestones were employed.

Relatively little innovation in castle design took place for a full century following the Conquest. This did not indicate either peace or complacency. The times were fraught with trouble but the castle-makers were evidently confident in the defensive capabilities of the available lay-outs. Normally the upgrading of a castle involved its translation from timber to stone. Eventually, however, the refinements of the techniques of attack germinated doubts in the minds of the castle-building classes and a long period of innovation and improvement was launched.

Chapter Five

The well-preserved keep at Conisbrough.

THE CASTLE AT WAR

The castle was a defensive weapon built to secure a territory and its overlord against invasion and insurgency. For most of the time it was likely to stand ungarrisoned and exist as a greedy drain on the resources of the owner and his estates. But in times of trouble every penny invested will have been deemed well spent – and many a lord must have gazed from his battlements and hoped that any skimping on the defence budget would not be the cause of his downfall. As a static defence system the castle posed a challenge to all those engaged in mobile offensive warfare. Human ingenuity guaranteed that weapons of attack would be devised which eventually could crack almost any existing stronghold. Anyone engaged in castle design needed a sound grounding in contemporary offensive warfare and a good imagination. He had to envisage the likely and the possible courses of an attack and produce effective safeguards. All who were associated with castles must have been haunted by the thought that no stronghold was stronger than its weakest facet, and both attackers and defenders needed to know where these weak spots lay.

As the castle became more massive and sophisticated, so it became more expensive and exclusive. Members of the Norman host taking possession of their new estates could have a motte-and-bailey castle cast up and palisaded for next to nothing, using only the sweat of their tenantry and the resources of their woods. Even an important royal castle like the one at Dover could be created in about a week, and in 1068 the Conqueror had castles erected at Warwick, Nottingham, York, Lincoln, Huntingdon and Cambridge – all completed within a few months. But evolution was expensive. When Henry II had a modern castle built at Orford in Suffolk in the years around 1170 it cost him £1400 – enough to support a family in comfort for more than a century.

It is estimated that in 1200 England and Wales together contained 400 castles, compared to around 1000 castles existing in the Norman period. (At present the sites of more than 700 mottes and 200 ringworks of the period between 1066 and 1215 are known.) A rather different assessment of numbers was provided by Hugh Braun in *The English Castle*, Batsford (1936), when he wrote:

> I once endeavoured to make as complete a list as possible of all the castles in this country of which traces could be found either on the ground or in documentary records of various dates. I came to the conclusion that there have been at some time or another on different sites in England some fifteen hundred

castles, of which perhaps seven-eighths were of eleventh- or twelfth-century foundation. In addition there were possibly two hundred or so in Wales, most of them of early date.

A more recent tally by D. J. King suggests that about 1700 castles were built in England and Wales and 700 of these sites display visible masonry.

Apart from their expense, the numerical decline in castles was also the result of strict royal control on the proliferation of baronial strongholds. During the anarchy of King Stephen's reign the building of vast numbers of adulterine castles caused great anguish, as revealed in an entry in the Anglo-Saxon Chronicle in 1137.

> . . . they filled the land with castles. They cruelly oppressed the wretched men of the land with castle works and when the castles were made they filled them with devils and evil men and they said openly that Christ slept, and His saints.

Not all these civil war castles were completed and the remains of one can be seen at Burwell in Cambridgeshire. In 1143 Geoffrey de Mandeville launched a violent revolt and harried the fenlands. King Stephen ordered that a chain of castles be built along the margins of the Fens to contain the rebels and at Burwell a great rectangular moat was dug. With a contempt for common people that was characteristic of the time, the castle was not built on open ground but a street of village houses was torn down to make way for the works. In the event the castle was never finished. De Mandeville attacked the building site and was mortally wounded in the skirmish which followed. He was shot in the head by an arrow, having removed his helmet and hood of mail. Contemporary records show that people at the time thought it strange that so feared a man could be slain by so trivial a weapon.

On securing his throne in 1154 Henry II was resolved that adulterine castles would be destroyed and that the imbalance between royal and baronial castles, then at a ratio unfavourable to the monarchy of about 5 to 1, should be reduced. It was during this reign that the keep underwent an important phase of evolution. At first Henry favoured 'traditional' square designs, like Appleby and Scarborough, and even in 1170 the keep at Newcastle was built square. Progress was represented by the unusual cylindrical keep with square towers at Oxford, the decagonal form of the Orford keep of 1173 and the mighty buttressed cylinder of Conisbrough of 1178. Later in the Middle Ages private houses were fortified but all such developments required the grant of a royal license to 'crenellate'.

Private castles were established as the hubs and strongholds of vast estates but the great magnates of the time did not spend their time cloistered within castle walls. Many held fragmented and widely scattered estates and their life consisted of a locust-like progress from manor to manor, with the aristocratic host consuming the local produce and slaughtering the game before moving on. Meanwhile the castle or castles would be left in the charge of a few domestics. Periodically the magnate and his family would return to the castle to preside at a great occasion, to entertain and enjoy the amenities of their principal residence, but even then the castle would not be garrisoned. When war came, however, it would be transformed and feudal tenants from the surrounding estates would be conscripted to perform military service for their lord. The nature of this tenure by 'castle guard' seems to have varied from place to place. Normally guard duty was required for about a month but in the case of some of the larger royal castles a permanent garrison was maintained. At Dover this numbered twenty-two or twenty-three knights, while sections of the perimeter were assigned to particular tenants. Their names are still commemorated in towers like Godsfoe's Tower and Crevecoeur's Tower. Occasionally documents survive which describe the stationing of particular tenants: one could do worse than Torphin fitzRobert of Manfield, who performed castle guard at Richmond in the fourteenth century and was responsible for the station between the brewhouse and the kitchen. After the middle of the twelfth century those burdened with castle guard duties tended to commute the service to a money payment. In times of peace the feudal superior was likely to settle for a fairly modest sum, but in wartime he would either charge a very high rate to tenants seeking to escape their military service or insist upon their presence in the garrison. Occasionally a castle would be abandoned and allowed to decay, but the lord would still charge his tenants a rent in lieu of castle guard. As the money economy became more strongly established so castles were garrisoned by wage-earning soldiers rather than by feudal service. In Plantagenet times a knight would earn around 8d per day and a sergeant about half this sum.

Private castles served partly as residences and were the aristocratic status symbol *par excellence*. Their distribution does not provide us with any great insights into the political geography of the medieval world and frequently they simply stood at the spot where the new foreign lord chose to build his motte. Royal castles were rather different, for they established and reinforced the royal presence and power across the surrounding territory. Most were occasionally visited by the king and were left in the charge of a lieutenant. Some were established to guard the vulnerable frontiers of the realm and a few dominated coasts or harbours. The pattern of royal castles reveals that no part of the realm could truly be deemed safe, for a while a minority of the castles anticipated foreign threats, most were concerned with internal security. No monarch could be sure that a great provincial lord or his heirs would not suddenly raise a rebellion or that a war between provincial dynasties would not erupt to offend the peace of the realm. The king's interests were spread throughout his kingdom, and so were his castles.

In military terms the role of the castle was that of holding territory – and to the medieval mind land was the source of all status and wealth. If a castle fell then its owner lost control of the territory which it guarded – and if it fell to a foreigner then his king was also the loser. In this way the castle was an instrument of defence, though it could be used in an offensive strategy to secure territory conquered in a military advance. Thus when William Rufus (1087–1100) invaded Cumberland in 1092 and annexed the territory from the Scots, he built a castle at Carlisle to secure his gains. Though Henry II strove to regulate the number of private strongholds there were times when the defence of the realm required private castles. In 1200 Henry's son John commanded his tenants in the March of Ireland to fortify their castles against insurgents, and those who failed to obey faced forfeiture. The strategic weakness of a castle derived from the fact that its garrison was likely to be much less numerous than the opposing forces, so that the scope for offensive forays was limited. If the attackers chose not to play the game and bypassed a castle rather than laying siege to it, there was little that could be done to prevent the harrying of the lands around.

The castle was in many ways a creation and consequence of feudalism. It is certainly true that a very hierarchical class system, a form of feudalism and a constant threat of war existed in Saxon England, but they existed without generating castles. The system in which castles became a crucial part of government originated on the Continent in the latter days of the Carolingian Empire. At the top of the hierarchy was the king who was owed the direct allegiance of his vassals-in-chief. These vassals had their own vassals and so the system of obligations was extended downwards through all society. Land was notionally deemed to be the property of the monarch and was let and sublet to tenants of diminishing stature. In return for the rents and services exacted the feudal superior was presumed to offer protection to his vassals, while all vassals of substance owed military service to their superior. In theory the system formed a stable hierarchy of obligations which converged at the apex of the feudal pyramid upon the king. In practice it was unstable, for it produced an armed and armoured society which was likely to fall into division and strife whenever central government was weak, or was thought to be so.

Henry I was well aware of these facts and used every available means to raise the revenue necessary to build his great royal keeps at Norwich and Rochester. A king's resources, however, had to spread across his kingdom while the great provincial magnate could afford to concentrate wealth in a particular dynastic stronghold. Thus the fortress of Aubrey de Vere at Hedingham or that of Geoffrey de Clinton at Kenilworth were equal to anything that the king might create. As we have seen, Henry II greatly strengthened the royal portfolio of castles and Edward I (1272–1307) used the castle as the key component in the pacification of Wales. In 1322 Edward II (1307–27) began to entertain doubts about his popularity amongst the barons and he issued an order for his royal castles to be provisioned and garrisoned. The English castles which received the command were as follows: in the west, Exeter, Bridgewater, Bristol, Gloucester and Sherborne; in the south-east, Rochester, Hastings, Leeds and Dover; in East Anglia, Norwich, Colchester, Clare and Pleshey; in the Midlands, Elmley, Warwick, Ludlow, Bridgnorth, Redcastle, Hodnet, Horsley, Donington, Tutbury, Cambridge, Melbourne, Nottingham, Newcastle-under-Lyme, Lincoln, Newark, Sleaford, Banbury, Somerton, Bolingbroke, Northampton, Oxford, Oakham, Marlborough, Windsor, Wallingford, Rockingham, Kimbolton and Devizes; in the north, Bolsover, Brough, the Peak, Pickering, Pontefract, Scarborough, Conisbrough, Sandal, Tickhill, Lancaster, Skipton, York, Knaresborough and Scarborough; and in the Welsh Marches, Denbigh, Beeston, Holt, Hereford and Hanley. When these English castles are considered along with the eight massively expensive castles built in Wales by Edward I it is clear that the defence of the realm – or more particularly, the defence of the throne – was an immensely costly operation at the start of the fourteenth century.

Centuries had elapsed before the balance was tipped conclusively in favour of the monarchy. Once the new balance was established, the feudal fortress simply withered away. The wars of Stephen's anarchy were castle-centred wars which hinged upon the cracking of defensive strongholds, the issue being settled in Stephen's favour, so it was believed, by the successful siege of Farringdon Castle. This experience, combined with those of the crusades, nurtured a castle-dominated mentality which endured until the costs of both attacking and defending a castle became insupportable. Expensive sophistication resulting from the competing offensive and defensive technologies eventually exceeded the resources of the deepest private pockets. In consequence the Wars of the Roses (1455–85) were largely determined by mobile warfare and pitched battles. The Tudor monarchy had the deepest pockets and could support a field army large enough and for long enough to starve out even the grandest private fortress.

Those engaging in castle cracking had a formidable repertoire of devices at their disposal. The early motte-and-bailey castles with their timber palisades might be taken by storm, but no sane force would run headlong into a stone wall. By the twelfth century the siege had become the cornerstone of offensive strategy. The development of siege technology partly involved rediscovering the methods current in Roman times and partly the assimilation of lessons learned by crusaders following the first experience of eastern siege devices in 1096. In 1097 crusaders took Nicea on the road to Jerusalem by igniting the timber props inserted in a gap quarried in the base of a tower. In the following year Antioch was besieged and taken by treachery.

Walls had to be got over or got through – but first it was necessary to gain access to the wall base. As often as not this required assailants to traverse the surrounding moat. This might be wet or dry, depending upon the permeability of the subsoil, the height of the water table and the availability of suitable streams for diversion. Wet was best, though not always possible. The attackers would attempt to build a causeway across the moat by filling a section of the trench with bundles of brushwood and baskets of earth. Manning the battlements would be a garrison of archers. They were more likely to be armed with crossbows – adopted in Europe early in the twelfth century – than with longbows, for although the crossbow had a slower rate of fire its 'quarrel' or bolt was lethal at a range of 300 yards (c. 275m) or more. In three years between 1210 and 1214 (one year's account is missing) some 109,000 'quarrels' were made by ironworkers at Knaresborough alone, at a cost of £78, which gives some idea of the popularity of the crossbow. As the attackers attempted to bridge the moat they would be caught in a hail of bolts, each bowman on the battlements being served by a boy who cranked and loaded the crossbow. Meanwhile the attackers would bring forward their own bowmen and hope to sweep the walls clear of the defending archers. Often the bowmen would advance behind a wheeled wooden shield or 'pavise'. The battlements of medieval castles could seldom be as heavily manned as Hollywood suggests. At Framlingham, for example, the 56-man garrison of 1216 allowed only four men per tower and wall section. Even so studies show that this was sufficient to cover the southern approaches completely. Experiments at White Castle, near Monmouth, showed that longbows could be fired effectively through arrow slits and that there was hardly any ground which was not covered by defensive fire. They also showed that it was easier than one might imagine for attacking bowmen to shoot these archers through their arrow slits.

When a castle was dressed for war temporary wooden hoardings or 'brattices' could be constructed on the outer sides of the parapets, allowing the defenders to fire downwards on those assaulting the wall base. The hoardings were built on stout beams thrust out through the walls to serve as brackets to support a boarded walkway, with a side screen and roof to intercept missiles. It is not clear how frequently brattices or warheads were seen on British castles, though they certainly appeared on some. In 1241 Henry III ordered such a hoarding to be erected on the Tower of London. It was to be built of sound timber and covered with lead so that '. . . people can look even into the foot of the said tower, and ascend and better defend it if need be'.

Once the causeway across the moat was ready the castle itself could be attacked, but first the assailants might try to ignite the brattices with flaming arrows or with fire pots launched from catapults. The commander then had to choose whether to launch a force over or through the walls. If he chose the high road then the choice was between using scaling ladders or a more elaborate machine known as a 'belfry'.

A belfry was a great wooden tower built to stand higher than the walls of the castle concerned. It ran on great wheels, was hung with wet skins for fireproofing and was topped by a drawbridge arrangement which could be lowered to allow the attackers to storm over the battlements. Before it was brought into action a track of logs was built to carry it across the moat and up to the wall base. Belfries could not be transported across the narrow, rutted tracks of the kingdom but were prefabricated close to the siege site. When Edward I laid siege to Bothwell Castle in 1301 he had a belfry built nine miles (14km) away in Glasgow and thirty waggons were used to carry the components to the castle. The journey took two days and a bridge was built for the crossing of the Clyde, along with a 'corduroy road' of logs. Such belfries were enormous structures; one of the two employed by Henry III in the siege of Kenilworth Castle in 1266 could accommodate 200 men. In order to succeed with such direct methods of assault the attackers had to bring the machine successfully to the castle walls and then launch a force sufficiently large to overwhelm the defenders massed on the ramparts. A great tower known as a 'bear' was built as a platform from which archers could fire on defenders manning the catapults, though at the siege of Kenilworth the catapults accounted for the bear.

Alternatively, an artillery attack might be employed in an attempt to batter down the castle walls and, in addition to his belfries, Henry deployed eleven catapults firing large stone balls at Kenilworth. Like the belfries or penthouses, similar artillery engines were employed in Roman times and were used in an attack on Syracuse in 215 BC. By the time of the crusades catapults of immense power which were operated by teams of men had developed. One, known as the 'Bad Neighbour', succeeded in battering down part of the city wall of Acre in the siege of 1189–91, where another large catapult or 'petraria' is said to have killed twelve men with a single huge stone missile. Such artillery engines could also be deployed by defending forces. At the siege of Jerusalem in 1099 the defending Turks built copies of the engines employed by their attackers. These were established on the city walls and used to fire flaming torches of pitch-soaked rope at the catapults and belfries of the crusaders.

If a much closer assault on a wall was to be mounted employing a battering ram then it was necessary to build a very resilient structure known as a 'sow' or a 'cat' to shield the operators from the rocks and incendiaries dropped from above. The ram might be directed at a gate if one was accessible, otherwise the efforts would be concentrated on a corner angle in the hope that the pounding of the ram and the prising of crowbars would dislodge masonry and undercut the walls above. A slower but sometimes more effective technique involved the use of mines. Sappers would dig a horizontal shaft until it reached a position directly beneath the castle walls. Here the tunnel would be stabilised with timber props around which inflammable material was heaped. When the props were ignited the support for the walls above was removed and an attack was launched to coincide with their collapse. The only defensive counter-measure available was the digging of a shaft to intercept the offensive mine, and if this was achieved then a frantic underground battle between the rival forces of sappers would result. During the siege of St Andrews Castle in 1546 the defenders heard the sound of picks wielded by advancing sappers; a counter-mine was dug and the attackers were slaughtered. Remains of both mines can still be seen. With the threat of mining in mind it was preferable for a castle to stand directly upon a hard bedrock. Where the ground beneath was soft, some protection could be gained from a deep moat and a high water table, for attackers would be obliged to tunnel beneath the moat while waterlogged subsoil would flood any mine.

Two of the most famous English sieges occurred within a couple of years of each other. In 1215 King John laid siege to Rochester Castle which had been taken over by rebel barons. First siege engines were employed in an attempt to pound down the walls, but the defenders took a heavy toll of their assailants. Then miners breached the curtain of the bailey and the rebel forces were driven back into the Norman keep. This was then attacked by miners at its south-west corner angle but the rebels continued to launch counter-attacks. Weakened by starvation the garrison finally surrendered after having endured a three-month-long siege. A year later the rebels encouraged the French to attack the royal stronghold at Dover. Powerful siege engines were brought to bear on the walls but the garrison maintained a resolute defence, even when told of the death of their king. A gateway in the outer curtain was breached but the walls within held and the siege was raised. To insure against future attacks on this weak point beak-shaped stone spurs were built in the breach and the access to the castle was moved with the construction of the great Constable's Gate.

Chapter Six

*Pembroke Castle showing
the well-preserved round
keep, left.*

THE CASTLE EVOLVES

During the second part of the twelfth century lords and warriors who had slept soundly within the walls of their great stone keeps may have begun to feel uneasy. Castles which seemed to all intents and purposes impregnable were now threatened by new advances in siege technology. The only insurance against such threats was to recommence building in a manner which would resist the engines and ingenuity of any foe.

There are at least two views current concerning the evolution of medieval castles. The most widespread sees a ruthless Darwinian process at work, whereby the castle was obliged to evolve apace with the technology of offensive warfare or face the horrible prospect of falling to an up-to-date siege army. Another school of thought argues that the preoccupation with the improvement of weapons is largely a modern phenomenon rooted in the very rapid 'improvements' in the machines of war which have taken place in the last century or so. It is argued that a basically strong and well-sited castle could expect to survive even if it had been overtaken by developments in warfare. There are certainly examples of castles which put up a good defensive show long after their military usefulness might have been thought to have passed and several seemingly decrepit castles were garrisoned and refurbished during the Civil War (1642–49). Bolton Castle in Wensleydale was a palace-fortress built around 1379. It was designed more for comfort and opulence than defence and overlooked by higher ground. During the Civil War it was garrisoned for the king and modern Parliamentary artillery battered at its north-west tower. Nevertheless the garrison maintained a stout resistance before surrendering in November 1645.

It is plain that castle designs were modified to take some account of current offensive thinking, though the degree of modernity or traditionalism displayed in a particular example could vary considerably from case to case. The authorities still disagree about the extent to which experiences gained in the course of the crusades as opposed to domestic warfare inspired the changes. When the crusaders campaigned in 'Outremer' they encountered a civilisation which was in many respects more advanced than the one that they had left behind. However, it has been argued that if the lessons in military architecture had been imported from the East then they would have been expressed in castles built after the first crusaders returned to Europe at the start of the twelfth century rather than in the second half of the century. Also, it can be argued that many of the sophistications could have been inspired by a study of the Roman strongholds whose ruins studded the towns and countrysides of Western Europe, and the Saxon shore forts with their walls punctuated with round artillery bastions.

The most important developments were designed to keep attackers, particularly sappers and engineers, away from the wall base. One innovation which is generally thought to derive from crusading experience was the adoption of 'machicolated' wall walks. Here the wall walk projected outwards from the top of the wall and openings in its floor allowed missiles and incendiaries to be dropped on those attacking the base of the wall. In Britain, however, stone machicolation was generally adopted only in the latter part of the thirteenth century and seems to have evolved from the timber brattices built in times of war and described in the preceding chapter. At Caldicote Castle in Gwent one can see the joist holes used to house the brackets supporting timber brattices and at Warwick Castle stone machicolations ring Caesar's Tower. Machicolation, whatever its origins, was not a revolutionary innovation for the most deadly and life-consuming weapons employed in siege confrontations were simply stones or boulders dropped from the battlements on to the heads of attackers.

More important was the adoption of the concept of the tall curtain wall which was regularly studded with towers. These towers projected outwards from the wall and thereby allowed the wall base to be swept with flanking fire of a sufficient intensity to drive away all but the most carefully shielded attacking forces. One of the earliest expressions of this important concept took place at Dover during the 1170s to 1180s with the building of a wall around the inner bailey armed with fourteen mural towers. At Dover the wall surrounded a keep of strong but traditional design. At Framlingham in Suffolk, however, the castle was rebuilt around 1190, an early example of a castle without a keep, the armour of masonry being concentrated in the curtain wall and its towers.

The first castle at Framlingham was built by Roger Bigod at the start of the twelfth century and was probably of the old ringwork and bailey type with a timber palisade crowning the ringwork. In 1175 Henry II ordered its destruction, after Hugh Bigod had participated in a rebellion. However the family recovered favour and Roger Bigod, second Earl of Norfolk, undertook the building of a stone castle which followed the oval course of the former ringwork. The curtain wall was built about 40 feet (12m) high and 8 feet (2.4m)

The curtain wall and wall towers at Framlingham.

thick and was studded with thirteen towers which projected a further 20 feet (6m) above the battlements. No keep was included in the plans but a hall was built inside the walls against the west curtain in the position now occupied by the seventeenth-century poorhouse provided by Pembroke College.

One of the wall towers has an irregular pentagonal plan but the remaining towers are all rectangular. In this way Roger Bigod anticipated the popular concept of making a curtain wall with mural towers the main defensive component of the castle, but he did not succeed in disposing of the weaknesses of rectangular structures with corners that could be undermined.

At this time the keep was by no means regarded as a redundant defensive structure and some interesting developments in thinking can be traced at Helmsley Castle in Yorkshire. In the years around 1200 Robert de Roos adopted a design based on a keep which was incorporated in the north-eastern wall of a moated, roughly trapezoidal enclosure defended by straight curtain walls with towers at the corner angles and flanking the northern gate, while the southern gate had a rectangular gatehouse. A rectangular tower was incorporated into an angle in the middle of the south-west curtain. The wall towers at Helmsley were made to a more advanced design than those at Framlingham, for instead of being rectangular in plan they were built round and so presented no vulnerable angles to attackers. The keep was also of an unusual design, neither circular nor rectangular but shield-shaped in plan, with its rounded face projecting outwards through the curtain. This side of the keep has been lost, for it bore the brunt of the Civil War siege in 1644. Many of the other remains of the original stone castle have been lost and today the most imposing feature is the strong barbican built around 1250.

Skenfrith Castle in Gwent has another innovative design, built about the same time as Helmsley as a replacement for an older motte-and-bailey stronghold. The River Minnow fed the wet moat and the stone curtain walls roughly followed the line of the earlier palisade. The keep, three storeys in height, stood upon the original motte but its foundations were sunk right down to bedrock level. It carried the development of the keep plan a stage further than at Helmsley, for a circular design was adopted. Surrounding the keep, the four curtain walls traced out a trapezium with four circular angle towers projecting to guard the wall base against assault. The circular keep at Conisbrough was built a couple of decades earlier and its six massive buttresses gave it a more distinctive appearance. Around 1190 this massively powerful castle was strengthened still further with the addition of a stone curtain wall to the bailey. This wall was punctuated by six semi-circular towers of solid masonry, one of the very earliest applications of the new rounded principle.

One of the most frequently visited castles built in this period, that of the mighty William Marshal, can be explored in Pembroke today. The round keep at Pembroke was massively built to a height of 78 feet (24m) with walls some 15 feet (4.6m) thick. It had four storeys and still retains its domed stone roof and two tiers of battlements.

The inner bailey was built about the same time to supersede the palisade of the earlier motte-and-bailey castle, and although the curtain wall has largely gone we know that the entrance was flanked by a semicircular tower. A much larger area of the promontory guarded by the water of the Pembroke river and the Monkton Pill was secured when an outer bailey was enclosed by a new curtain wall with circular towers around 1250.

Although English historians have tended to accept that the progress towards scientifically designed castles derived from crusading experiences, several French academics give much of the credit to English monarchs, most notably Henry II. Certainly the fortifications at Dover and at Windsor, where the upper ward curtain was rebuilt with rectangular wall towers around 1170, both anticipated the direction of castle development and served as prototypes for new designs in England, Wales and the continent of Europe. These castles, those earlier described at Conisbrough, Framlingham, Helmsley, Pembroke and Skenfrith, and others at Orford, Berkeley, Farnham and Chepstow all helped to indicate the directions for advance in design, not only in Britain but on the Western European continent as well.

The crucial adoption of projecting towers providing platforms for flanking fire would have had little significance but for the rise to prominence of the bowman as a leading figure in the defence of a castle. As bows had not been highly regarded as defensive weapons, when the earliest stone castles were built they were not equipped with loopholes. Primitive crossbows may have been known to the Norman conquerors, who, perhaps unusually, included a force of conventional archers. Crossbows were considered barbarous weapons and were banned by the Church (if ineffectually) but crusading experiences revealed the potency of the crossbow, a fact underlined when Richard I (1189–99) was killed by a bolt wound which turned gangrenous. In April 1199 he had been prancing outside Châlus in Limousin where a golden Roman relic which he wanted was held. A crossbowman took pot shots at him and he congratulated him on his shooting. Then he misjudged the flight of a bolt and England was well rid of one of its more foolish kings.

The crossbow was valued by both sides in any castle-centred confrontation. The attackers would use it in their attempts to clear the battlements of defenders while these same defenders would employ similar weapons to keep the operators of siege engines, battering rams and the much feared belfry at bay. The crossbow was an important influence in the adoption of mural towers and the provision of loopholes, embrasures or 'crenelles' in battlements, which were largely absent in earlier castles. When the keep at Pembroke was built around 1200, numerous slits to accommodate bowmen were provided.

The evolution of the keep was a more hesitant process. The concept of the mighty tower as a focal stronghold was deeply embedded in the thinking of the Normans and their successors. Thus when Richard I developed his immensely costly state of the art castle at Château-Gaillard in Normandy in the last years of the twelfth century, a tower keep was a vital component of the layered defences. Earlier French castle-builders had grappled with the weaknesses presented by rectangular keeps and experimented by providing small turrets on the corner angles to overlook what would otherwise have been dead ground. The potential of such innovations was scarcely explored in Britain, where the emphasis came to lie on building the entire keep to a circular or polygonal plan. The earliest English example of a round keep is at New Buckenham in Norfolk. Various writers have pointed out that many flint church towers of the period in this area were built circular but this simply reflects the fact that the region was far from any sources of good building stone which could be exploited to provide corner stones or 'quoins'.

The keep at New Buckenham stands inside a ringwork and dates from around 1140. It was a private castle of the d'Albini or Daubigny family, who also held the hall keep at Castle Rising. It existed as an unbuttressed cylindrical tower and stood a good 20 feet (6m) higher than the present ruins of its lower level. The castle withstood a siege in the 1260s and was held against the king's officers by Alice Knyvett in 1461 during her husband's absence but was slighted during the Civil War. Despite its revolutionary form this round keep does not seem to have influenced castle design, though those built towards the end of the century at Conisbrough, Pembroke and Skenfrith certainly did.

According to the historian D. J. Cathcart King, English tardiness in exploring the possibilities inherent in the circular tower can be traced to the lack of royal initiative. Royal castles generally led the field in the adoption of innovations and were often models for other castles but Henry II's great keep at Dover was a massive rectangular structure in the traditional manner. Earlier, in 1165–72, the royal castle which he built at Orford had adopted an unusual and original plan. The keep was built as an eighteen-sided polygon but this potentially influential design was marred by the addition of three square towers, which served as buttresses and housed the staircase. He also built an octagonal keep with a square turret to house the staircase at Chilham in Kent about a decade later, but it was left to an illegitimate brother, Hamelin Plantagenet, to point the way forward with his castle at Conisbrough, a private castle like those of New Buckenham and Pembroke. Perhaps a factor which delayed the adoption of the round form concerned the inconvenience or loss of accommodation resulting from attempts to provide rectangular rooms within a circular plan. Eventually, however, the round design took root and was applied to great castles and also to the less illustrious strongholds which became quite numerous in the troubled Welsh countryside.

Powerful earls like Hamelin Plantagenet and William Marshal contributed greatly to the advance in castle design, as did another mighty earl, Hubert de Burgh, Earl of Kent and Justiciar of England. He was responsible for redesigning the approaches to Dover after the almost disastrous French siege of 1216 and he applied his experience to his castle at Montgomery. Hitherto the locality had been guarded by the motte at Hen Domen, described in Chapter 4. In 1223 the defensive focus was moved and a natural rocky knoll was exploited. The contours of the site required an elongated enclosure and strength was concentrated in a massive gatehouse tower established at the southern end of the ward. It was built four storeys high with three great chambers at different levels above the long entrance passage. Two great drum towers projected from the outer face of the gatehouse and a guard room lay to one side of the entrance. The strength of the design was soon put to the test, for in 1231 Llywelyn the Great's army burned Montgomery but failed to take the castle. When de Burgh fell from grace Montgomery became a royal castle and in the middle of the century the site was strengthened by walling the outer ward in stone. Montgomery, however, existed as a member of a new generation of castles, for the Norman castle-building tradition had reached the end of its evolutionary development.

The castle built by Henry II at Orford

Chapter Seven

M odern interest in castles focuses on their role in medieval warfare and castle visitors like to imagine the old walls decked out for war and ringed by hostile armies. In reality a castle might exist for a century without a single arrow being fired from the battlements and some castles never experienced a siege. From time to time the castle became a bastion and haven of defence, but usually it was home to its noble owners and to some of their domestics and retainers. As explained, it was unlikely to be the only home of an aristocratic family. Some, like the Daubignys, had more than one castle and most would spend much time touring their subordinate manors, while the king only visited the royal castles occasionally.

The unhomely qualities of most genuine castles have often been stressed. Certainly most readers, if they could be transported back across the centuries, would find the lives of even the loftiest members of the castle-dwelling classes to be almost intolerably uncomfortable. For a start, we lack resistance to many of the bugs which medieval folk could usually shrug off, but we would also consider the furnishings of the castle appallingly primitive, the sanitary arrangements disgusting and the cold and dark intolerable. Since we might also find the main pastimes barbaric and the social life uncouth the romance would soon wear away from our visions of chivalry. However, it is hardly reasonable or relevant to compare castle life to modern conditions and values and when we compare the castle to its domestic alternative, the unfortified manor house, then the castle does not fare too badly. When we compare life in the castle to that endured by the hovel-dwelling peasants who made up the vast majority of populations of all medieval countries then the castle re-emerges as a palace of privilege.

The degree of comfort in castle life depended on the period concerned, the affluence of the owner and the degree to which the castle was an armoured outpost in hostile territory or a well-appointed abode which might occasionally hear the call to arms. William the Conqueror, in the most snug setting that he knew, could never have imagined the luxuries enjoyed by nobles of the second or third rank living in castles of the fifteenth century. And when fourteenth-century kings left the luxuries of a favoured abode such as Windsor Castle to tour the outer provinces they would find the facilities to be far more rough and ready. There was also a contrast between the relative security of life in a grand castle of the English heartlands and the general state of armed readiness experi-

PREVIOUS PAGES
The Norman hall at Hedingham.

enced in the turbulent marchlands of the Welsh, Scottish or Irish territories. Gentry of a modest status resident in Suffolk or Berkshire for example, would have aspired to no more than a timber-framed manor house with just a status-claiming moat to keep trouble at bay. But those living around the fringes of the Welsh uplands would spend their domestic life in the cold, constricting confines of a tough little castle. A few small castles were of a purely martial nature, built to maintain a foothold in dangerous territory, and in such places any comfort was sacrificed to the demands of war.

In a medieval king's absence his castle was normally placed under the authority of a resident constable. In 1205 Nicholas de Stuteville was unable to meet the 'inheritance duties' or 'relief' levelled against him by King John, which amounted to the stupendous sum of 10,000 marks (more than £6000). In setting such a high sum John may have been seeking to gain control of Knaresborough Castle to establish a royal presence in territory dominated by hostile barons. If so, the ruse succeeded and John installed one Brian de l'Isle as constable in the new castle. De l'Isle had begun his career as an obscure knight in the royal service but rose to become one of the king's leading lieutenants. Under his guidance Knaresborough became one of the main royal strongholds in the north and a fortune was lavished on its defences. But de l'Isle was strictly accountable to his master; he was not a lord in his own right and regularly submitted financial details to the king.

To understand the castle we must try to see it through medieval eyes. Feudal society was a martial society. It embodied arrangements whereby the feudal superior could call upon the armed support of his inferiors, and was bound together by obligations of loyalty. Men of status perceived themselves as warriors – a dangerous phenomenon in any society. Today the oddballs and inadequates who are infatuated with weapons and imagine that they will be able, given only a nuclear holocaust, to emerge from obscurity and become survivors in the Rambo mould are one of our smaller problems. However, a society whose leaders are virtually all preoccupied with conflict and feats of arms is a society for ever teetering on the brink of war. When the castle owner went to war his shield, banner and surcoat were emblazoned with his personal arms. All could see how he behaved on the field of battle, and if he was lucky some troubadour might compose a verse or ballad to perpetuate his valour. When he entertained his peers the talk was likely to focus on the deeds of heroes past and present. When he played the countryside became a killing field. And when he died he was buried beneath a tombslab which did not advertise his intellect or virtue but portrayed him fully armoured and accoutred for war.

It would be hard to imagine such a man living in a house that did not reflect the martial values of the age and did not proclaim the status and might of the dynasty dwelling within. As civil strife was gradually eradicated from the realm, the comforts were increased and the castle was domesticated. Already, however, the most favoured of the royal castles had demonstrated how splendid and opulent living could be within the shelter of armoured walls.

The Normans had precise ideas about the lay-out of the residence of a family of substance, ideas which can be discovered by exploring one of the several surviving unfortified Norman stone houses. The ground-floor level accommodated a vaulted undercroft which was used mainly for storage and access to the floor above was gained via an external stone staircase. The greater part of this floor was occupied by the hall. This was a large public room where the lord performed his many public functions. It was the administrative and legal hub of his estate, a place for eating and entertaining, and when the feasting was over the guests would sleep upon its floor. The existence of the castle as a frequently bustling centre of hospitality is evidenced by excavations at Weobley Castle, Birmingham, which showed that the floor of the corridor leading to the kitchen was renewed six times in the course of a couple of centuries. The private domestic life of the noble family had a secondary importance and was enacted in a smaller room at first-floor level, the solar, which was a bedroom-cum-sitting room. Probably because of the fire risks involved the kitchen was sometimes housed in a separate building. This simple lay-out was modified and assimilated into the Norman tower keeps. These buildings were usually more than two storeys high, but in all of them the great hall retained its pre-eminence. As in the undefended house the hall was normally placed at first-floor level and reached by an external staircase, though in a few cases, like Newcastle, the hall was at second-floor level. At Newcastle the stairs were defended by a 'forework' built against the outer face of the keep and guarded by three towers. The tallest of these towers contained an anteroom through which visitors hoping to meet the king in his hall would have to pass, and as royal visits to Newcastle were infrequent this room normally served as a lodging for the king's constable. The King's Hall occupies most of this level, a huge rectangular chamber equipped with a capacious fireplace. When the king entertained his court and the local nobility here the room would have been organised in the established manner. At the head of the room the king, his family and main dignitaries would be seated at the high table. Other guests in descending order of importance would be seated at trestle tables running down the chamber at right angles to the high table.

When the king had his fill of food, entertainment and conversation he could slip away into his private chamber or solar which adjoined the hall. Here he had two luxuries: a fireplace and a lavatory. The lavatory or 'garderobe' was a draughty and unsophisticated little chamber which discharged through the outer wall. A second garderobe was available for guests in the great hall. The queen had a similar solar provided on the floor below, but arranged in such a manner that access was only via the king's suite, thus reducing the risk of gossip and scandal. On the opposite side of the hall to the solar was a well room. All castles were naturally obliged to have their own self-contained water supply, and at Newcastle the well plummets through the tower and downwards into the ground to a depth of 100 feet (30m). The kitchen would have existed as a timber structure jutting out into space from the wall of the well chamber. Thus in the royal keep at Newcastle the essential Norman houseplan of a hall flanked at either end by a solar and a kitchen was replicated at second-floor level. At first-floor level was the Queen's Hall and apartments, while the uppermost floor was the province of the garrison. The ground-floor level of the keep, like that of the unfortified house, existed as a stone-vaulted storeroom. Since castles often stored the surplus production of the surrounding estate and had in any event to be provisioned for war, the storage space required was considerable. Frequently the gloomy, oppressive undercroft is mistakenly regarded as a dungeon. The keep at Newcastle was furnished with two prisons, one in the south-west corner of the basement for less prestigious offenders and another for more distinguished internees in a corner angle at the level of the King's Hall.

The smaller keeps were less elaborate but certainly no more homely. There was no forebuilding to guard the entrance, which was reached either by an external stone staircase or by a ladder which could be hauled up in troubled times. The basic arrangement of a great hall standing above a vaulted undercroft was preserved, but in some cases an extra upper storey was obtained by rationalising the roofing arrangements. Originally many keeps were roofed in a steeply-pitched gable or twin gable. Such a timber-built roof was very vulnerable to ignition by fire arrows, so that the roof was set low and screened by the four towering walls. The adoption of lead sheet roofing removed the fire risk and allowed flat roofs to be built at battlement level, so that an extra accommodation level could be inserted into the space previously occupied by the gable.

As standards of living and hospitality increased, so too did the demands for space.

The hall keeps in which the internal space was divided by a main partition wall provided much more practical accommodation than did the tiered tower. In due course, the shift in emphasis towards the curtain wall allowed much more flexibility and space in the provision of domestic rooms. The lengthiest retinue of retainers, officials, statesmen and hangers-on was, inevitably, the one which accompanied the king on his perpetual rounds. Consequently it was at the royal castles that the demand for more and more apartments was most keenly felt, though the pressure also affected those high nobles offering hospitality to the royal party. In one case at least the desire to impress the monarch backfired. When the de Veres entertained Henry Tudor (1485–1509) at their ancestral Hedingham Castle the king was served by flunkeys gaudily clad and wearing the white star emblem which the family had adopted in distant crusading times. Because the king had recently imposed a ban on all such private liveries as part of his policy of constraining the power of the barons his hosts received a hefty fine.

Since the castle was usually not only the defensive focus of its territory but also the organisational centre, the activity increased apace with the growing complexity of administration. Again this feature was most prominent in the royal castles, for those which commanded county towns were each occupied by the king's leading local government official, the sheriff. Normally the sheriff had his office in the castle and the great hall was used as the venue for the shire court.

The castle's massive walls of stone must have stored the chills of winter and, as defence prohibited the building of windows larger than the merest slits, most chambers were gloomy as well as cold. Draughts were another unwelcome feature of castle life. Window openings were seldom glazed and doors might be ill-fitting. Sometimes interiors were, for reasons of security, set out in such a manner that one could not reach a private chamber without cross-

(Opposite)
Dunnottar Castle is thought to occupy the site of a Pictish promontory fort.

(Overleaf)
Conway Castle.

Beaumaris Castle.

Harlech Castle.

ing a public one, so that the draughts would easily circulate around a building. Despite these severe restrictions it is clear that considerable efforts were often made to improve home comforts. To improve lightness and sanitation walls were limewashed. This treatment was sometimes applied to the outside of castles too, hence the naming of London's White Tower. Tapestries could be hung on the walls of the great hall and solar and some rooms were more imaginatively decorated. For example, Queen Eleanor, the wife of Henry II, had her chamber at Windsor wainscoted and painted green with gold stars. Henry was a more fastidious king than most of his predecessors and he complained about the sanitary arrangements at the Tower of London:

> Since the privy chamber of our gardrobe at London is situated in an undue and improper place, wherefore it smells badly, we command you on the faith and love by which you bounden unto us, that you in no wise omit to cause another privy chamber to be made . . . even though it should cost a hundred pounds.

The provision of furniture was extremely spartan by modern standards. Tables of the refectory type existed in the Middle Ages but many guests took their meals from heavy boards resting on trestles. A richly painted table of a smaller kind is known to have stood beside the bed of Henry III at Winchester Castle. There were benches lining the tables but chairs were not plentiful. From contemporary illustrations it appears that the leaders of society possessed chairs with X-shaped frames like modern camp stools, which folded and could accompany the lord on his progress around his estates. When entertaining in his hall the lord was literally the chairman, for he sat in glory on the dais on a canopied chair of heavy oak. The furniture in the hall was robust if unsophisticated, and in wartime the wall benches and table would serve as platforms for archers. There were no cupboards or chests-of-drawers and all items of value were stored in oaken chests. These were neither objects of elegance nor were they particularly well designed, for it was not until the middle of the fifteenth century that carpenters developed the technique of framing loose panels to allow for the shrinkage of timber. By this time a form of cupboard known as a 'hutch' had also been developed for use in the solar where its purpose was to store food for snacks. It was during the Tudor period that private funds were released from the calls of defence and could be invested in 'luxuries' like specialised pieces of crafts-man-made furniture.

The medieval desire for a well-appointed home is best represented by surviving documents relating to the royal castles, and it is clear that the arrival of the host was often preceded by a frenzy of improvement and prettification. King John demanded ovens at Ludgershall and Marlborough large enough to accept two or three complete ox carcasses. The consequences flowing from a royal visitation can be judged from the preparations made for the celebration of Christmas at Winchester in 1206. King John commanded the sheriff of Hampshire to obtain one hundred pigs; one hundred sheep; twenty oxen; 1500 chickens and 5000 eggs. (And so it is not surprising that when King John met his timely end in 1216 the cause was said to be dysentery aggravated by a surfeit of peaches and raw cider!) Where royal castles were concerned the visitation was a costly event. For example, when King John visited his castle at Knaresborough in 1206 the accounts record the importation of twenty large barrels of the king's wine from Boston and when he hunted in the Forest of Knaresborough in 1210 accommodation had to be found for more than thirty of his hunting dogs, the dogkeeper and his assistant. The concern for comfort extended outwards to the precincts of the castle. Henry II had a garden set out which he could view from his apartments at Arundel; Henry III had a cloistered lawn at Windsor and Edward I had a fenced lawn laid outside Queen Eleanor's suite at Conway.

Other outdoor facilities were of a more practical nature. Since the consumption of meat was banned by the Church on up to three days of the week, artificial fishponds were highly valued because they provided a reliable alternative source of protein. Carp appears to have been the fish most frequently raised in the ponds and these ponds normally had several compartments with the young fish being netted and moved from one to the next as they matured. Dovecotes were also frequently found in the vicinities of castles, the young birds being gathered from the nesting niches which covered the interior of these buildings.

Most medieval kings had a passion for bloodsports. Kings controlled the hunting rights in the extensive – but by no means continuously wooded – royal forests and some castles, like the one on the motte-and-bailey site at Laxton in Nottinghamshire, were the administrative and legal foci of particular forests. Meanwhile the leading nobles and churchmen sometimes hunted in their private chases. A more certain and amenable outlet for blood lust was provided by the release of deer from a confined deer park. These ditched and stockaded enclosures proliferated in the earlier medieval centuries and around 3200 examples existed by 1300. Most castle owners had easy access to a nearby deer park and the royal palaces at Woodstock and Clarendon were particularly well served. Hunting was not merely an outlet for male aggression in an age of violence. The women of the castle-dwelling classes engaged in archery, falconry and ferreting and in 1221 Henry III allowed the Abbess of Barking to go foxhunting in Havering Park.

Entertainment of a more dangerous kind was provided by tournaments. These did not necessarily resemble the stylised jousting which, according to Hollywood, was a perpetual activity in the medieval castle yard. The diversion was introduced from France in the twelfth century and began as violent and largely disorganised mayhem in which participants were frequently killed or captured and held to ransom. As the popularity of tournaments increased to a level where the peace of the realm was seriously threatened, in 1194 Richard I licensed and regulated the events, restricting them to five open sites, the locations of which are now only loosely known. And as the tournaments became more closely controlled, they became more stylised and much less lethal. In the later medieval centuries 'tiltyards' for jousting were established at various castles, though most have vanished leaving little if any trace. At Kenilworth Castle, however, it is known that the fifteenth- and sixteenth-century tiltyard occupied a narrow causeway and dam which separated two artificial pools at the main approach to the castle.

Many readers will regard the outdoor pursuits of the medieval nobility as bloodthirsty and brutish. These people did lead very active outdoor lives and not only did the exertions and fresh air intensify the appetite for the gargantuan feast, they must also have ensured that the participants arrived home too tired to be over sensitive to the discomforts of their abodes. On the whole the feudal magnates were active people and their castles, when they were in residence, were active places. Recreation, administration, courtly romance and courtly intrigue did not leave one with too much time to brood on the chills and gloom of castle life.

The castle visitor will find that it is seldom easy to interpret the domestic suites in a crumbling building. With no children playing in the nursery, cooks at work in the kitchen or ladies gossiping in the bower the places seem cold and dead. Several castles do, however, preserve the framework of rooms within which many generations of medieval family life were enacted. At Richmond there was an unusual arrangement whereby the eleventh-century hall stood separate from the keep. The two-storey building is an important survival and consists of a great hall standing above a storage basement or undercroft. From the great hall there is access to a small solar which stands above the arched entrance to the outer ward. The building is known as 'Scolland's Hall', the name commemorating a man who was responsible for performing castle guard here.

Manorbier Castle, near Pembroke, preserves its nucleus of a hall and tower dating from the start of the twelfth century. Many of the elements of Lord de Barri's home and setting – the church, mill, fishpond, park and dovecote – can still be traced. Later the castle became celebrated as the birthplace of the Welsh chronicler Giraldus Cambrensis (Gerald of Wales), born here in 1146. He was fond of his home and described the castle as he knew it with pride:

> It is excellently defended with turrets and bulwarks, and is situated on the summit of a hill . . . having on the northern and southern sides a fine fishpond under its walls, as conspicuous for its grand appearance as for the depth of its water, and a beautiful orchard on the same side, enclosed on one part by a vineyard, and on the other by a grove, remarkable for the projection of its rocks and the height of its hazel trees. On the right hand of the promontory, between the castle and the church, near the site of a very large lake and mill, a rivulet of never-failing water flows through a valley . . .

This description shows that even a castle of the twelfth century could be the sort of place that one was loath to leave. As time progressed so the accommodation became more and more elaborate. One of the last private castles to be created was built at Caister, near Great Yarmouth, in 1433–48 by Sir John Fastolf, the model for Shakespeare's Falstaff. His design was inspired by his extensive campaigning experience in France, but instead of building a massive stone structure of traditional design he chose to work in brick. He built it on the site of the family's old moated homestead, probably living in Blickling Hall during the early building phases. The building ranges followed the margins of two rectangular courtyards which were linked by a drawbridge and were completely surrounded by a moat. The castle featured a great tower and curtain walls but it paid full regard to the latest domestic expectations. There were about forty separate chambers including staterooms for Sir John and his wife, two halls, a chapel, armoury, brewhouse, bakery, kitchen, larder, cellar, buttery, pantry, numerous storerooms and stables. Amongst Sir John's suite of rooms was a room which reflected the new opulence of castle life: a 'stew' or bathroom equipped with bowls, bath and water tank. The Great Hall was festooned with lavish tapestries depicting religious subjects, sporting scenes, recreation and warfare. Walls were plastered and painted, the main rooms were even carpeted, while fireplaces and garderobes were in generous supply. Windows at the higher levels were large and embellished with painted glass, though timber shutters were fitted in case of attack. There is no doubt that any Norman castle owner would have regarded Caister as a palace of unimaginable luxury and it certainly marked an important stage in the march from stronghold to mansion.

Though a late-comer to the martial ranks, Caister was a castle as well as a palace. Soon after it was built it was inherited by the Paston family, but the Duke of Norfolk arrived with an army of 3000 men, turned them out and surrendered it to the crown. He said it was '. . . a fair jewel, and the king should as soon have his life as that place'.

Chapter Eight

*Some of the formidable
defences at Conway.*

THE QUEST FOR PERFECTION

During the twelfth and thirteenth centuries the castle underwent a period of sustained improvement and sophistication, culminating in the magnificent and seemingly impregnable fortresses created in the reign of Edward I. The days of the ditch, bank and palisade would seem to have been left far behind – though in fact a lack of time and money obliged Edward to build just such an old-style castle at Linlithgow in 1302. Increasingly, however, the emphasis was placed on the scientific development of defenceworks and the adoption and elaboration of successful innovations.

As we have seen, the age of the stone keep was succeeded by an emphasis on the curtain wall and mural tower. At first the wall towers were relatively unsophisticated, as at Framlingham, but it was soon appreciated that if towers were built as virtual keeps then each could be defended even if the walls were scaled or breached. By the thirteenth century the lessons of Dover and Framlingham had been assimilated and developed so that cylindrical towers were a conventional feature of new castle works. The picture book castle had come into being.

The early thirteenth-century castle at Montgomery, previously described, had much of its armour of masonry concentrated in its gatehouse. Early experiments with mighty gatehouses can be seen at Arundel and Exeter and at Dover the inner bailey, built by Henry II, had its two gateways guarded by close-set pairs of mural towers. In due course the entrance flanked by towers evolved into a single mighty gatehouse building, as exemplified by the castle at Tonbridge. Not only did the gatehouse concentrate strength at what would otherwise have been the most vulnerable point on the defensive perimeter, it also constituted a refuge in its own right, a place that could still be defended if the wall was breached or if part of the garrison revolted. With the development of such a strongpoint and command post the role of the traditional keep was usurped, so that the typical great castle came to exist as a series of strong towers linked by a formidable and continuous curtain wall which converged on a mighty gatehouse.

Many exercises in castle improvement took place on sites already fortified, so that instead of producing a state of the art design the builders were obliged to work within the constraints imposed by existing defenceworks. Where strongly curving sections of ramparts were concerned, as with those of old ringworks, several towers were needed to cover all the pre-existing blindspots along the perimeter. Often motte mounds were prominent components of the old design and these might acquire a round tower. Clifford's Tower at York stands upon a mighty motte, one of two built here by William the Conqueror to dominate the town and river. Until the middle of the thirteenth century the crown of the motte was palisaded, the timber being renewed on several occasions. In 1245 a stone tower was built upon the motte, not to a simple circular plan like the ones built on mottes at places like Cambridge or Hawarden in Clwyd, but to a unique quatrefoil plan like a four-leafed clover. Later the tower gained its name from the rebel baron, Roger de Clifford, whose body was hung in chains from the walls of the tower in 1322. The Clifford family carried out their own progressive castle works at Skipton, where the site was probably previously fortified by a more primitive walled enclosure. Built in the early part of the fourteenth century the castle was D-shaped in plan, with a straight wall to the north defending the crest of the cliff overlooking the River Aire and with six linked towers defending the semi-circular enclosure which faces southwards. Two of these towers bracketed the gateway and formed a gatehouse, subsequently masked by a later entrance.

Impressive as Skipton Castle was, it was already outshone by the remarkable strongholds built in Wales for Edward I. Where the sites allowed, these Edwardian castles were built to a concentric plan involving walls within walls. The roots of the concentric lay-out are to be found in the tendency to wall the outer bailey once the inner bailey of a castle had been embraced by a circuit of walls. Outer bailey defences had normally been less substantial than those of the inner ward, but they did protect the less important outbuildings and also helped to keep attackers away from the inner defences so long as the outer ward could be held. Purpose-built and scientifically designed, concentric defences involved rather more than just defending an inner and an outer ward with towered curtain walls. The two layers of defence were set close together with the battlements and towers of the inner wall overtopping those of the outer walls. This arrangement allowed the archers manning the top of the inner wall to fire down over the heads of their comrades on the outer wall – and it equally allowed them to sweep the lower ramparts with arrows if attackers were able to gain control of the outer wall. The space between the two walls was not an outer bailey of the traditional type and it did not contain buildings such as barns and stables associated with the peacetime life of the castle. Instead

*(Opposite)
Dunvegan Castle, Skye, home of the chiefs of the clan MacLeod for 700 years.*

it was a narrow gorge between the great walls in which any force that had cracked the outer defences were exposed to the missiles and counter attacks of the garrison.

The most perfect example of a concentric Edwardian castle is Beaumaris on Anglesey, which was added to the king's clutch of North Welsh castles to guard the northern approaches to the Menai Strait. Work was begun in 1295, but although it continued for thirty-five years it was never completed, leading to the truncation of most of the towers. However, the level seashore site eliminated any need to take account of irregularities of terrain and it was possible to accomplish an uninhibited concentric layout. The moat defined an octagonal plan which was followed by the towered walls of the outer bailey, built in the second decade of the fourteenth century, long after the building of the inner bailey. A small sea dock intruded into the southern side of the moat. The inner bailey was built to a square plan with circular angle towers, D-shaped towers projecting from the midpoint of the eastern and western walls and great gatehouses in the northern and southern walls. The walls were built to a thickness of almost 16 feet (4.9m). When the gateways in the outer bailey were built they were set a little out of line to the gatehouses to allow flanking fire to be directed at any force heading for the entrances to the inner bailey. The gatehouses were the strongholds within the stronghold and each entrance was defended by three portcullises and two doorways.

At other Edwardian castle sites the terrain considerations produced some less symmetrical applications of the concept, but at Harlech symmetry also prevailed. The castle at Harlech was built between 1285 and 1290 on a knoll overlooking the sea (the shoreline having since advanced very considerably) with a massively strong inner bailey that was rectangular in plan with circular towers at the angles. This was surrounded by the less formidable walls of what was in effect a middle bailey. On the south and east side there was a wide moat, while the approaches to the west and north were enclosed by an outer bailey. The difficult rocky terrain guarded the castle on three sides, but the east front was vulnerable so strength was concentrated here in a great gatehouse with walls that were more than 12 feet (3.7m) thick in places. Facing the gatehouse was the bridge over the moat, which had drawbridges at either end and which was exposed to concentrated fire from overlooking walls.

Caernarvon Castle had a less regular plan, resembling a thickly waisted hour glass with the inner bailey forming the western

(Opposite above)
The gaunt ruins of Corfe Castle.

(Opposite below)
Nappa Hall in Wensleydale with its pele tower.

component and the outer bailey the eastern one. The circuit was defended by nine wall towers and two gatehouses. One was at the eastern extremity of the castle and the other, the King's Gate, provided the entrance to the town built to accompany the castle and stood facing the moat at the junction of the bailey. (Originally it was intended to extend this mighty structure all the way across this junction.) The whole fortress was commanded by the great Eagle Tower, a keep-like structure at the western extremity of the complex. The castle was built to be defended by a large garrison of archers and provision was made for the defences to be manned by up to three tiers of bowmen, some of them able to shoot in three different directions. Caernarvon was designed to be the most impressive of the Edwardian castles in Wales, for in addition to its defensive duties it was designed to serve as a seat of government and a palace for the Prince of Wales. Impress it certainly did, and when the commentator John Taylor saw it in 1650 he was moved to write:

> I thought to have seen a town and a castle, or a castle and a town: but I saw both to be one, and one to be both: for indeed a man can hardly divide them in judgement or apprehension: and I have seen many gallant fabrics and fortifications but for compactness and completeness of Caernarvon I never yet saw a parallel. And it is by art and nature so fitted and seated that it stands impregnable; and if it be well manned, victualled and ammunitioned, it is invincible, except fraud or famine do assault, or conspire against it.

The plan of Edward's great castle at Conway was partly dictated by the rock upon which it stood and, like Caernarvon, it consisted of two baileys placed side by side and enclosed by a strong wall punctuated by circular towers. The larger of the two baileys contained the king's Great Hall and the administrative buildings of the garrison, while the smaller housed the royal apartments.

All these castles were built as integrated components in Edward's strategy of obliterating Welsh resistance, which became concentrated in the rocky fastnesses of Snowdonia. They were made possible by the presence of a strong and purposeful king who was able to draw upon substantial state revenues. The sophisticated defensive principles embodied in these works, which included the construction of more than one strongpoint and alternative inlets for provision in the event of siege, were in many cases anticipated by the castle built at Caerphilly in 1267–77. However, when Edward began the first of his Welsh castles at Flint in the year of Caerphilly's completion, he used a less progressive design. The plan was that of a rectangular walled enclosure with a circular tower projecting from each corner, the southern tower being much larger than the others and surrounded by its own moat. This tower embodied the concept of a keep, a concept which was already out of fashion. In this application, though, the keep tower played an innovatory role, for a gallery inside its walls allowed defenders to escape a force which had broken into the strongpoint and then to circulate around the wall passage and take their enemies in the rear. Edward seems to have based his castle at Flint on the one which he had seen as a crusader at Aigues Mortes in Provence.

At the same time that Edward commenced his works at Flint the task was begun at Rhuddlan, close to the site of the Saxon *burh* of *Cledemutha* (described in Chapter 3), and at Aberystwyth. Little remains of the latter castle, though the inner ward appears to have been lozenge-shaped with gatehouses placed at opposed corners. Rhuddlan is still majestic and was built to a concentric plan which is less obvious today because of the removal of most of the outer curtain wall. Great twin-towered gatehouses were placed on two of the angles of the square inner ward, while the other two angles are guarded by large round towers. Here and at Flint the work was supervised by James of St George, who became Master of the King's Works and was responsible for the great projects at Caernarvon, Conway, Harlech and Beaumaris.

Edward I built a total of fourteen castles around the borders of North Wales. These were Flint, Rhuddlan, Ruthin, Caergwrle, Builth and Aberystwyth, which were begun in 1277; Conway, Harlech and Caernarvon, begun in 1283; Denbigh, Hawarden, Holt and Chirk, begun after 1284; and Beaumaris, begun in 1295. In addition, the battered castles which had been held by Welsh princes at Dolwyddelan, Criccieth and Castell-y-Bere were repaired and rebuilt. Space does not permit us to look in detail at all these castle works, but Harlech presents a well-documented case.

In the December of 1282 the Prince of all Wales, Llywelyn the Last, was killed near Builth and early in 1283 the Welsh castles of Dolwyddelan and Bere fell to English sieges. The fall of Castell-y-Bere allowed a force of 560 infantrymen led by Sir Otto de Grandison to press on through Merioneth to Harlech and work on the new castle began as soon as the force reached the coast. In the

June of 1283 a group of twenty stonemasons and quarry workers was despatched to Harlech from an English base which had been established at Conway following the fall of Dolwyddelan Castle. Their tools were loaded on pack horses and the journey across the rugged terrain of Snowdonia took two days. A second party of fifteen masons and a squad of carpenters were despatched in the following month. Steadily the workforce was expanded, so that by the summer of 1286 the working community at Harlech included 546 labourers, 227 masons, 115 quarry workers, thirty blacksmiths and twenty-two carpenters. The wage bill for the labourers and craftsmen amounted to nearly £240 per month. Before the work was suspended during the first winter of operations, the building of the main inner curtain wall was well advanced. This then provided a secure and defensible enclosure to protect the workforce in the event of a Welsh attack. The walls were raised to a height of about 15 feet (4.5m) and the final heightening of the curtain was not completed until 1289. In the second and third seasons of work progress was made on the great gatehouse and the adjacent rock-cut ditch so that at the end of 1285 accommodation in the gatehouse was available to Sir John de Bonvillars, Edward's constable and the Deputy Justiciar of North Wales. A garrison had been stationed there from as early as 1284 and consisted of the constable, thirty soldiers (including ten crossbowmen) along with a chaplain. Harlech's construction was directed by Master James of St George and in July 1290 he was appointed constable. He served in this position for three years while continuing his duties as Master of the Works.

Harlech Castle had not been finished long when it met its first challenge during the uprising of Madoc ap Llywelyn in 1294–95. At this time the sea lapped close to the walls of the castle, so that while isolated from the land by the siege party, Harlech could be victualled from Ireland by sea. The castle was tested again during the Glendower uprising and in 1404 it fell to the Welsh patriot following a prolonged siege. After its capture Harlech became the base of Glendower's court and government and it may have been here that he was formally crowned as Prince of Wales. At the end of 1408, and following another long siege, Harlech was recaptured by the English. The castle received such a sustained battering from the English artillery that much of the outer curtain wall was destroyed. During the Wars of the Roses Harlech was held for the Lancastrian cause and the castle fell for the third time to a siege mounted for the

Yorkists by the Earl of Pembroke, although again it did not fall *The gatehouse at Harlech.*
before displaying a stout resistance. After the Wars of the Roses the
castle seems to have fallen into neglect and such maintenance as
took place was only due to the fact that it provided the venue for the
Merioneth Assizes. During the Civil War Harlech faced its last siege
when it was held for the king by his constable William Owen of
Brogyntyn. Again the siege was long but ultimately successful and
the fall of Harlech marked the end of the war.

Detailed information is also available concerning the building of
Beaumaris Castle, the last component of the Edwardian series. In
the August of 1283 the king visited the manor of Llanfaes on
Anglesey which was held by his friend, the sheriff of the island

county, Roger de Pulesdon. It was probably at this time that the decision to build Beaumaris was taken. In 1294 a Welsh revolt against compulsory enlistment for service in Gascony was led by Madoc ap Llywelyn; Caernarvon was damaged and Roger de Pulesdon was murdered. The revolt was quelled in the winter which followed and then the population of Llanfaes was evicted and moved 12 miles away to a newly-established settlement called Newborough, built on the southern extremity of Anglesey. The Llanfaes site was commandeered for the building of the new castle and town of Beaumaris.

The direction of the building works was entrusted again to Master James of St George. Work began in the spring of 1295 and between April and September of that year the prodigious sum of £6502 was spent on the building works. Between 1295 and 1330 the costs of building amounted to £14,344. Most of the stone used at Beaumaris had to be imported by sea and the transport costs encountered were greater than those faced at Conway, Harlech and Caernarvon together. During the summer building season a work-force of around 1800 men was employed, which included about 450 masons and about 375 quarrymen. Among the items imported were 3277 boards, 2428 tons of sea coal for burning lime for mortar and 105,000 assorted nails. The early stages of the work involved erecting a barricade around the site to protect the workforce, excavating the moat and building the walls of the inner ward to a height of at least 20 feet (6m) so that gates could be put in position and locked at night. Work on the castle dock allowed vessels of 40 tons to sail laden right up to the castle gate at high tide. A transport fleet of 30 boats, 60 waggons and 100 carts was employed in assembling stone at the building site and in hauling coal to the lime kilns.

On 27 February 1296, James of St George and Walter of Winchester wrote to the officials of the exchequer at Westminster to report on the work and appeal for funds:

> . . . we have kept on masons, stone-cutters, quarrymen and minor workmen all through the winter, and are still employing them, for making mortar and breaking up stone for lime; we have carts bringing this stone to the site and bringing timber for erecting the buildings in which we are all now living inside the castle; we also have 1000 carpenters, smiths, plasterers and navvies, quite apart from a mounted garrison of 10 men accounting for 70s a week, 20 crossbowmen who add

another 47s 10d and 100 infantry who take a further £6 2s 6d
. . . we are short of £500, for both workmen and garrison. The
men's pay has been and still is very much in arrear, and we are
having the greatest difficulty in keeping them because they
simply have nothing to live on . . . we could not make do with
less than £250 a week throughout the season . . . In case you
should wonder where so much money could go in a week, we
would have you know that we have needed – and shall
continue to need – 400 masons, both cutters and layers,
together with 2000 minor workmen, 100 carts, 60 waggons and
30 boats bringing stone and sea coal; 200 quarrymen; 30
smiths; and carpenters for putting in the joists and floorboards
and other necessary jobs . . .

In the event the castle was never entirely completed and the king's
interest had become redirected towards Scotland. Relatively little
building work seems to have been achieved after 1295 though
urgent works were needed to meet the widespread fear of a hostile
alliance between the Welsh and the Scots. James of St George died
in 1309 and was succeeded at Beaumaris by Nicholas de Derneford.
The building work continued sporadically until 1331 when it finally
ground to a halt. From time to time the shortcomings of the
unfinished castle were pointed out and in 1539 attention was again
drawn to the threat of a Welsh and Scottish alliance. Richard
Bulkeley reported that: 'Conwey, Carn' and Hardlach castles have
nothing in them to defend them for one hour'; he observed that if
they fell into enemy hands '. . . it would cost his majesty a hundred
thousand of his pounds and the loss of many a man afore they
should be gotten again'. Anglesey, he warned, was but a night's
sailing from Scotland and he begged for '. . . a couple of gunners
and some good ordnance and powder to defend the king's house in
Bewmares'.

As at Conway and Caernarvon the new castle was accompanied
by a new town, in this case the successor to the nearby town of
Llanfaes, whose inhabitants had been deported. The borough of
Beaumaris was chartered in the September of 1296, and although it
was intended to be built as a walled town like Conway and
Caernarvon, town walls were not acquired until later. In 1315 the
burgesses unsuccessfully petitioned the king for town walls to be
built. However, it was not until the start of the fifteenth century,
following heavy destruction during the Glendower revolt, that a
wall was provided. Between 1403 and 1405 the castle and town

were in Welsh hands and the building of the wall seems to have taken place in the second decade of the century. Meanwhile Beaumaris had developed a lively commercial life to complement the administration activity which focused on Caernarvon.

Strategic considerations ensured that Wales received a disproportionately large share of the scientifically designed Edwardian castles, buildings which may be regarded as the pinnacles of medieval castle design. Scotland would be able to display other such castles of conquest had the funds available to the English crown not begun to dry up. The conquest of Wales was more durable than that of Scotland and Scottish castles started by Edward may have been destroyed during the Scottish resurgence, though the remains of a great gatehouse at Kildrummy in upper Donside are generally attributed to him.

The building of great fortresses in the second half of the thirteenth century was not monopolised by the crown. Gilbert de Clare began his magnificent castle at Caerphilly in the reign of the relatively weak monarch Henry III, and he enjoyed the independence of action available to English marcher barons. Edward I encouraged his powerful supporter Henry de Lacy, Earl of Lincoln and Salisbury, to begin a mighty castle at Denbigh in 1282. As at Caernarvon and Conway the castle was accompanied by a plantation town and was as much a part of the policy for pacifying Wales as were any of the royal castles. In some respects Denbigh Castle, with its massive curtain and multangular towers, was stronger than the royal castles. Its designer seems to have developed a preference for multangular towers over circular ones.

Towering above its surrounding rock-cut ditch, Goodrich Castle, to the south of Hereford and Worcester, is bound to enthral the visitor. It was built towards the end of the thirteenth century by Edward I's uncle, William de Valence. The old twelfth-century keep was incorporated into the rectangular castle which had round towers at three corners and a strong gatehouse in the north-eastern corner.

The castle building programme took place against an active and evolving background of war. The investment of much of England's wealth in the extension and control of its Welsh and Scottish frontiers led to a shortage of resources for the guarding of the invasion coast, so that at the end of the thirteenth century the French succeeded in burning Dover. Meanwhile the scale of warfare was growing to horrifying proportions which far outstripped the reserves of manpower obtainable by enforcing the traditional feudal obligations of military service. Increasingly there was a need for experienced professional soldiers, and vassals greatly preferred to substitute a cash payment for their martial duties. In this way the amateur armies of conscripts were replaced by great forces of hired mercenaries. In troubled times a castle was not staffed by familiar vassals and tenants but by a more permanent and substantial garrison of hired killers who were frequently loyal only to the highest paymaster. Not surprisingly the castle owner began to feel the need to watch his back; no castle was so strong that it could not fall to treachery. Such insecurities emphasised the importance of the keep gatehouse which could serve the lord, his family and his loyal retainers as a last redoubt against not only the enemy outside the walls, but also the enemy within. However, this development created problems of its own, for it was not always easy to reconcile the needs of defence and the conveniences of domestic life within a single building. Ultimately all such problems were solved when only the king could afford to maintain armies large enough to prevail. The barons must have regarded the decline of the private stronghold and the diminution of their powers with feelings that were mixed.

Chapter Nine

Caernarvon Castle.

THE BUILDING OF CASTLES

To build a castle one needed to be the king or to possess – at any rate in settled times – a royal licence to crenellate. One also needed a site, a workforce, materials and sufficient funds to pay for them. As castles became more massive and sophisticated, so the building costs escalated. In the course of the Middle Ages the situation in which anyone with pretensions to nobility would expect to have a castle changed into one in which very few people were wealthy enough to contemplate building a castle of the first rank.

While mottes like the one at Hastings were thought to have been cast up in very little time, a modern expert estimate suggests that the Norman motte at Castle Neroche in Somerset embodied 13,780 man-days of work and so would have occupied a ten-man force for about four years or a 100-man force for five months. Costs were incurred if the decision to build or rebuild in stone was taken. The stone had to be quarried, shaped, transported to the building site and assembled by a body of competent masons. All this was quite costly, and if the stone had to travel over a distance of more than a few miles then transport could be the most expensive item in the budget. The survival of medieval state accounts provides us with detailed insights into the sort of costs involved in building royal castles, although it is very difficult to translate the sums into modern values. The substantial stone keep at Newcastle took about eleven years to build and when it was completed in 1178 its construction had cost about £1000, a sum equivalent to around one-tenth of the total state revenue of the day.

Any subservient peasant possessed the skills needed to work on a motte-and-bailey building site, but most quarry work, the dressing of stone and the setting out and building of stone castles demanded more specialised skills. Among the obligations owed by Saxon tenants was that of 'burghwork' or labour on fortification sites, and this burden was exploited under Norman feudalism. Later in the Middle Ages masons and other workers needed for the king's works could be conscripted, willingly or otherwise, and directed to the site concerned, though they were paid their full wages. Both inflation and increasing sophistication were responsible for the sharply rising costs of castle building, and when Conway Castle was erected little over a century after the completion of the castle at Newcastle it cost about fourteen times as much. In modern terms its cost might be calculated at four to five million pounds, but to interpret such a figure we need to remember that the state revenue then amounted to a few tens of thousands of pounds, not the billions of pounds of today. Also, even with all the technological advances at our disposal we could not reproduce Conway Castle for such a modest sum. The records which have survived to itemise the costs of private castle building projects are far fewer, though work on the brick-built castle at Caister in the years 1432–35 amounted to about £1480.

When Edward I embarked upon his castle-building strategy in Wales he launched the most comprehensive programme of work seen in Britain since the building of the Roman forts of the Saxon shore. Little or nothing is known about the ways in which the earlier castles were designed, though it is sensible to suppose that they were planned by the king or noble who would foot the bill in consultation with the master mason employed and whatever experts on contemporary warfare were available to advise. Doubtless accountants also had a role to play. The Edwardian castles are different because they were, in effect, architect designed and something is known of the professional designer employed. 'Master James of St George' is now believed to have been called Saint-Georges d'Esperanche and to have been a native of Savoy. Before working in Wales he had designed castles in Savoy and with his appointment as Master of the King's Works in Wales he became responsible for the gargantuan building operations there.

The operations in Wales were of such a scale that they severely stretched the kingdom's resources of non-agricultural manpower. Castle building took place against a background of a great and sustained campaign of religious building involving cathedrals, monasteries and parish churches. This was the era of the decorated style, during which thousands of churches were built, rebuilt, extended and embellished with the fashionable but time-consuming flowing, naturalistic carving. Nobody who had acquired skills in the building crafts need ever have gone short of work. The masons, however, do not seem to have greatly exploited the demand for their skills. They were not highly paid and unlike some other craftsmen basking in the privilege of membership of an urban guild, the masons were peripatetic and knew little home life. Many seem to have originated in quarrying districts and to have begun to acquire their skills while working in the local quarries. Thereafter their lives were spent in moving from one building site to another, and at the end of their useful working lives there might be little to look forward to but the assaults of arthritis and silicosis.

Such men might at any time be conscripted by the king's officials and despatched as impressed labour to one or other of the royal fortress building sites. There is no doubt that castle building periodically seriously disrupted ecclesiastical building works and Ranulf of Higden noted that conscription of labour to work on Windsor Castle in the mid-fourteenth century had the effect that '. . . hardly anyone could have any good mason or carpenter, except in secret, on account of the king's prohibition'. Although the conscripts were paid according to the current rates it is plain that they were often reluctant recruits, and mounted sergeants were employed to prevent workmen from absconding from the building sites. These sergeants were paid 7½d (about 3 pence) per day, rather more than twice the rate paid to most craftsmen, while more labourers earned only about 2d (less than 1p) a day. At Caernarvon in 1304 no less than seventeen different rates of pay were current. The records show that in 1282–83 there was scarcely an English county which did not make a sizeable contribution of manpower to the projects. Yorkshire, for example, despatched 20 masons, 40 carpenters and 150 diggers and Lincolnshire sent the same.

In the course of twenty-five years Edward is calculated to have spent between £40,000 and £50,000 on his eight new castles in Wales. The castles were not built consecutively, for work on four different strongholds often continued in parallel, while five of the castles were accompanied by new-built towns. Although the castle at Conway was completed in just five years and Rhuddlan a little more quickly, work at Beaumaris took much longer and never did achieve completion. In 1295 the Justice of Chester was commanded to recruit 100 masons, complete with the tools of their trade, and despatch them to Caernarvon. By 1301 the works here had already cost some £16,000 and were far from complete, and in 1304 we know that four quarries providing stone for the site employed 33 quarrymen and that 53 masons were at work on the castle. The main Edwardian castles were accessible by sea and four royal vessels and a number of chartered ships were used to convey materials, such as timber, to the building site. Labour was costly in wages and it also had to be provisioned and the demand for food circulated widely. For example, during the building of Beaumaris the keepers of the See of Winchester were ordered to have 1000 quarters of wheat, 600 quarters of oats and 200 quarters of barley carted to Chester for despatch to the building site.

The availability of stone was a vital factor to be considered at the beginning of any project. If the local stone was soft, like chalk, then it was of no use. And if it was hard and intractable, like granite or basalt, then enormous energies would be expended in shaping it. Ideally one sought a workable stone which could easily be sawn and chiselled to shape and which would harden on exposure to the atmosphere. The best limestones, like those quarried by the villagers living in the shadow of the castle at Corfe in Dorset, satisfied these requirements, but became prohibitively expensive when a castle was any distance from the quarrying sites. When the Normans invaded, the English quarrying industry appears to have been poorly developed and high-class 'freestone' was shipped across the Channel from Caen at great cost. When used in Norwich Cathedral in 1287 a quantity of stone cost £1 6s 8d (£1.33) at source, but it cost £2 10s 8d (£2.53) to ship it to Yarmouth and then there were the added costs of moving it to Norwich by barge. Caen stone was used in the greatest southern churches, but when Henry II built his costly castle at Orford the budget would not stretch to

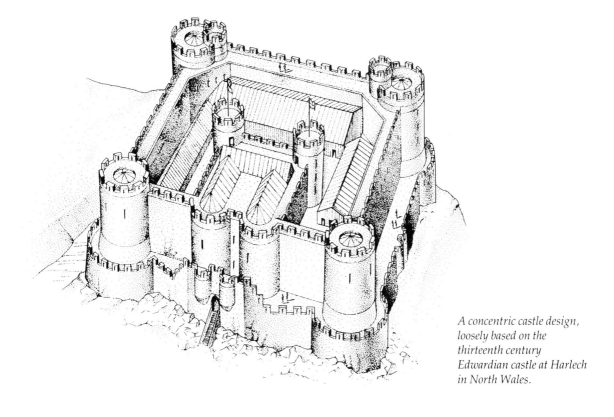

A concentric castle design, loosely based on the thirteenth century Edwardian castle at Harlech in North Wales.

allow such luxuries and the builders were obliged to quarry the poor local nodules of limey clay and marl. In the reign of Edward III materials as well as manpower were pre-empted for work on the most extravagant of all the royal castle works, when £51,000 was spent on improvements to Windsor Castle.

Castles needed to be strong but they did not need to be decorative. Consequently stone that would be shunned by the builders of cathedrals was acceptable to those who built castles and most medieval fortresses were made of locally quarried stone. Ludlow, with its walls of sandstone quarried nearby, was typical. Edward I was fortunate that the hard rocks of Snowdonia provided suitable building material for his castles. Often, however, stone suitable for walling was not good enough for dressings, lintels and mullions. At Harlech good freestone was brought from a site 8 miles (12km) to the south and some of the stone used at Rhuddlan was shipped all the way from Chester. Lime for mortar was imported to all castle sites except for a few situated on limestone outcrops. Where a castle was built of reasonable stone it was always likely to be pillaged for building materials once its useful life was over. The medieval chronicler Leland recorded seeing the last tower of Elmley Castle being broken up to provide stone for the repair of the bridge at Pershore, near Worcester.

Some of the last exercises in castle building were accomplished in brick, a material less tough than stone but more widely available and also redolent of high status. The bricks used in Caister Castle were made locally and brick was also employed in the great tower of Tattershall Castle in Lincolnshire, built in 1432–46. The brick clay was dug from pits a few miles to the north of the castle and in one year the castle accounts show that 384,000 large bricks and 84,000 small bricks were made. Kirby Muxloe Castle in Leicestershire was a fortified manor of the 1480s, built for William, Lord Hastings. Labour was attracted from many parts of the kingdom, including bricklayers from East Anglia, where much of the pioneering work with brick had been accomplished, the master bricklayers receiving 8d (just over 3 pence) a day, twice the wage of a labourer. However, the grand design was halted by the execution of the Yorkist Lord Hastings when Richard III (1483–85) came to the throne and his widow later resumed work on a much more modest scale.

Castle building works were controlled by the seasons and masons could find themselves deprived of work and income during the winter months. At Kirby Muxloe we know that carts were built

(Opposite)
The keep at Caldicot in Gwent dating from around 1200.

and draught oxen purchased in the winter of 1480–81 and these were used to import stone and bricks in the spring, when the foundations were laid. The master mason, John Couper, who had worked at Tattershall, was employed in May of 1481, along with the master bricklayer, John Hornne and the master carpenter, John Doyle. The three Johns and their workmen worked on the site until late in October, but during the winter the walls were insulated against the frost with straw until work recommenced in the following March.

Detailed information is available for the coastal artillery fort built by Henry VIII (1509–47), Sandgate Castle, near Folkestone, now destroyed by the sea. Work began in the spring of 1539 and accelerated in the summer, when some 500 workmen were employed, but during the winter season the numbers at work dropped to around 100. In June 1540 some 630 men were employed here and the castle was completed in the autumn of that year. Skilled stonemasons, bricklayers, carpenters and sawyers were paid 7d or 8d per day (about 3 pence), 1d to 2d more than the gunners in the garrison. Labourers, who were outnumbered by the skilled artisans, received a wage of 5d (2 pence) a day. In the June of 1539 nine men were jailed for leading a strike for higher pay.

The stone used at Sandgate was Kentish ragstone, which was quarried from the cliffs nearby. This poor-quality stone was supplemented by top-class freestone which had originally been imported from Caen in France and was pillaged from disused monasteries in the vicinity of Sandgate. An abandoned priory was robbed for lead and bricks and tiles were imported from kilns at Rye and Canterbury. Timber was obtained from the Weald but coal to fire the lime kilns which produced the mortar was shipped from the North of England.

Each castle that we see, and various great castles which have disappeared, like the ones at Bristol, Gloucester or Banbury, embodied an enormous amount of work. Walls that were ten or more feet thick consumed vast quantities of masonry, all of which had to be quarried and hauled to the building site. When we remember that the overwhelming majority of the population was composed of impoverished peasants it becomes apparent that castle building was a major consumer of the country's resources of energy and skill. No modern building programme can really compare with the castle works of the High Middle Ages, although defence remains the greediest drain on the nation's wealth.

(Opposite above)
The artillery fort at Deal.

(Opposite below)
Markenfield Hall, a fortified manor house.

Chapter Ten

The castle and town at Richmond, North Yorkshire.

CASTLE, TOWN AND COUNTRY

The prime strategic role of the castle was that of securing control of territory. Inevitably any castle had a great influence on the territory which surrounded it. In Norman times it might be seen as a glowering symbol of oppression. At other times and in other places it could be a source of security or a crucial market for the local economy. Many castles had an intimate association with a neighbouring town or village and sometimes the settlement concerned owed its very existence to the castle. Its role as a haven for the local populace in times of trouble was not clear-cut, for it must be remembered that in addition to its military role the castle was a dynastic residence and not a communal bolt-hole. In wartime it was provisioned to sustain a garrison and the castle owner would not wish to have the foodstocks eroded by non-combatants. But whether in royal or in private hands the castle was very likely to be the administrative centre of the locality and would provide a venue for the courts of justice.

The royal castle at Corfe was the administrative focus of the Isle of Purbeck. Each 'tithing', a group of ten households, in the district was obliged to provide a man to serve for ten days as part of the castle garrison and he would be paid the king's wages. The farms in the vicinity were required to supply a stated amount of grain and hay while other vassals and householders had to supply items from a wide range of goods – from poultry to horseshoes – or provide artisans like carpenters. The constable of this castle claimed rights to timber, stone and firewood, to a share of the beer brewed in the district and to commandeer carts to import supplies from Wareham. He could muster the local militia and, on the king's behalf, lay claim to all sturgeon, porpoises or falcons. In addition he was responsible for gamekeeping duties and for the licensing of boats and he even had the power to approve or prevent all marriages within his jurisdiction.

There are plenty of Roman and much earlier examples which show that a fortress would tend to stimulate the growth of a civilian settlement nearby. This did not only happen at great imperial foci, like York, but also at frontier stations and outposts, such as Housesteads fort on Hadrian's Wall or Bainbridge in Wensleydale. Where the early medieval castles are concerned it is not always easy to know whether the castle begat the village or the village acquired the castle. In some cases, as at Burwell, the archaeological evidence shows that the castle was inserted into an already flourishing village, but in others the lack of surface evidence and documents leaves one to wonder. There are also numerous cases where the settlement concerned is so obviously planned to a grand design that there is no doubt that the castle owner either built a village or town to accompany his stronghold or else largely remodelled an existing settlement.

Kilpeck in Hereford and Worcester is a virtually deserted village which would be almost unknown outside its county were it not for the magnificence of the carving which embellishes the Norman church. Visitors, who come from far and wide, may wonder why such expensive attention should have been lavished on a church in a remote setting exposed to Welsh raids. The answer is to be found directly behind the church, where there are the remains of the motte-and-bailey castle of William fitzNorman, whose grandson rebuilt the church in the first half of the twelfth century. The economy of the community was also stimulated by the establishment of a priory here in 1134. Today the earthworks of the departed village extend from the church and lie within crude earthen defences but a wonderful legacy of Norman carving remains as a memorial to the times when Kilpeck with its castle was a place of some note.

At Kilpeck the castle was added to an existing community with a Saxon church which was already old. At Bolsover in Derbyshire the situation was different though not unusual. Shortly after the Norman Conquest the manor acquired an earth and timber castle. Early in the twelfth century stonework was added and in 1155 the castle was forfeited to the Crown and subsequently developed to control the royal lead mines in the Peak District. Within a short time of the establishment of the earthen castle a planned townlet was established beside it, with a long high street and a rectangular market place which became triangular as the town encroached upon it. In 1225 a formal market charter was obtained and the town became established as a thriving commercial focus. The modern town still preserves the deliberate framework of early medieval planning, with its main street extending along a limestone ridge to the south-east of the old castle site and with old side streets, lanes and property boundaries still in use.

The medieval trinity of castle, town and market is repeated time and again, and not far from Bolsover there is Castleton, dominated by the stone keep of Peveril Castle and retaining a portion of its planned market place. Medieval planning on a grander scale can be recognised at Ludlow. The stone castle was begun by Roger de Lacy in 1085 and enlarged in the following century as well as in the fourteenth and sixteenth centuries. The town of Ludlow was probably created by the de Lacys as soon as their castle was built. Like most other castle towns, it was set out to a plan, with its broad High Street running eastwards from the gates of the castle and made sufficiently wide to accommodate a market. Outside the castle, market stalls lined the street and in course of time they evolved into shops. The plantation town became firmly established and successful and by the close of the fourteenth century it was a place of some importance with more than 1000 households. Indeed, it proved more prosperous than any of the other castle towns established in the Welsh Marches, many of which were virtually stillborn or doomed to obscurity.

One such was Cefnllys. The Mortimers, a leading family of the Welsh Marches, established a castle here in the 1240s and the town was founded in an old hillfort site. A century later only a score of burgesses had established themselves here; the settlement did achieve borough status by 1360, yet before the century had ended the number of burgesses had halved and subsequently the place became deserted. The antiquary Campden described Cefnllys as a lovely ruin at the end of the sixteenth century but it endured as a rotten borough with the occupants of three farms and a cottage returning a Member to Parliament until early in the nineteenth century.

The establishment of plantation towns in Wales and the Welsh Marches was a deliberate instrument of royal and baronial policy in the Middle Ages. It was hoped that the planting of alien, mainly English, commercial communities in countrysides threatened by Welsh insurgency would strengthen the English hold on the territory and might encourage more settled attitudes amongst the Welsh. But the attractions of the castle town were by no means confined to political matters of pacification, and new towns were established in the most stable of localities. Such towns and villages could accommodate feudal tenants and supply various useful goods and services to the garrison. The greatest appeal, however, derived from the benefits of market trading, for the lord who controlled a thriving market derived a considerable income from the collection of market tolls and fines. No lord would tolerate a situation in which the commerce of his estates was unregulated or dominated by 'forestallers' who traded before reaching the appointed market. Medieval markets were licensed or chartered by the crown and all lords anxious to increase their revenues would hope to control settlements with a busy chartered weekly market and the bonus of at least one annual fair capable of attracting the greater merchants with their more sophisticated and exotic wares. Such successful trading would often exist far beyond the shadow of the lord's castle, but the presence of a castle and garrison would stimulate the market and strengthen the authority of the lord. However, the wealth and standing of the lord did not necessarily grow apace with that of his market. If trading increased the prosperity and numbers of the commercial population beyond a critical point then the burgesses could be expected to attempt to purchase a borough charter from the crown. When they succeeded they obtained the right to organise their own affairs and were exempt from feudal interference. In this way in the course of the Middle Ages the town emerged as a symbol of freedom.

When a castle town succeeded and expanded, its growth might or might not mask the patterns of medieval planning, while when it failed, as at Cefnllys, its outlines might only be marked by bumps and hollows in the pasture. In some cases neither a marked success nor an abject failure disturbed the passing years, so that the outlines of the medieval vision remain faithfully preserved. This is the case at New Buckenham, near Diss in Norfolk. William Daubigny inherited a castle at Old Buckenham, but chose to build a new one on a different site, possibly because it dominated a once important thoroughfare from Bury St Edmunds to Norwich. (The unusual circular keep of the castle has already been described in Chapter 6.) Close to his castle he founded the market town of New Buckenham, which was set out to a grid street plan with a market green filling one of the squares of the grid. A common where the new townsfolk could pasture their livestock was provided beyond the town, and the fact that rights of pasture were given for eighty cattle has led to the suggestion that, as originally laid out, New Buckenham contained eighty house plots. Fortune neither frowned nor smiled on Daubigny's creation, and although a church was built in the thirteenth century and a delightful market house in the seventeenth, and while the houses standing on the tenement plots have undergone several complete rebuildings, the outlines of New Buckenham are still very much as Daubigny created them more than 800 years ago.

In cases like New Buckenham the relationship between lord, castle and town becomes clear to anyone familiar with the characteristic clues. However, the story is much harder to unravel when a town was deliberately created but where an irregular lay-out was adopted or where later expansion and rebuilding have hidden the traces of planning. Knaresborough Castle was probably established in the 1120s and in 1169 there is a first reference to the existence of a colony of burgesses. These people would be freemen who were encouraged to establish themselves here as craftsmen and traders and charged only the most modest rents of 1d (0.4 of a new penny) per year. The later growth of the town, which housed eighty-six families of burgesses by the start of the fourteenth century, and the encroachment of the town over part of its old market place have masked the original lay-out. It is likely, however, that the early town had an expansive market area which reached right up to the ditch surrounding the castle. Such an open space fronting the castle was desirable because it deprived attackers of cover. The free burgesses would have lived around the other flanks of the market, while a ghetto for the unfree population of bondsmen lay further away at 'Bonds End'. The town was protected by a modest ditch and rampart, but this was of little value when Knaresborough was invaded and almost completely burned by the Scots in 1318.

Of the eight new castles which Edward I built in Wales, five were accompanied by purpose-built fortified towns. These castle towns were designed to fulfil several roles. It was thought that by establishing urban centres of commerce the indigenous people would learn from the example and be enticed to adopt more peaceful and prosperous lifestyles. The burgesses who were settled in the new towns were largely of English origins and so the policy established alien populations around the heartland of Welsh resistance. And the towns had useful roles to play in association with their neighbouring castles. Their markets drew in foodstuffs needed to support the garrisons and they also provided accommodation for administrators associated with the castle.

Flint and Rhuddlan were the first of the Edwardian castle towns. Building began in 1277 and both towns took about four and a half years to complete. Flint was built to a neat gridiron plan and was surrounded by a ditch which joined the castle moat. There was no town wall but a rampart and palisade. Large numbers of carpenters were employed in building the timber houses of Flint and some of these houses were burned during a Welsh uprising in 1282, just after the town's completion. But Flint survived, and the medieval lay-out of parallel streets is still preserved in the townscape.

At Caernarvon, where work began a year after the completion of Flint, the defences of the new town were much more impressive. The site commanded the Menai Strait and its military advantage had been recognised by the Romans, whose fortress of *Segontium* was nearby. Work on the castle did not begin until the town defences were completed, which then guarded the northern landward approaches to the fortress. The western side of the town faced the waterfront and the semicircular site was surrounded by walls studded with eight half-round bastions. Within these defences a gridiron plan of streets was set out. By 1298 fifty-six English burgesses had taken up occupation of 'burgage plots' inside the town and a further six had taken half plots. In less than two decades the population had doubled and the town had spread beyond its walls. In addition to the plots which the townspeople occupied within the walls, they also enjoyed rights in the surrounding farmland. This was not unusual, for many medieval townspeople devoted some of their time to agriculture.

Denbigh was taken from the Welsh prince Dafydd ap Gruffyd in 1282 and Edward granted the site to the Earl of Lincoln. A plantation town was created beside the site of the castle works and in 1290 the forty-seven burgage plots were all tenanted. As at Caernarvon, the burgesses were also allocated holdings of farmland but each was obliged to join the garrison if required or to provide an armed man as a substitute. The six burgesses who had taken double plots were required to provide two armed men. The new town, which occupied a walled hilltop site beside the castle, was stormed by the Welsh in 1294 but was subsequently reconstructed. In 1468 Denbigh was violently destroyed during one of the encounters of the Wars of the Roses and as the town recovered there was a drift of townspeople away from the original walled site to a new extramural location on the northern flanks of the hill.

Not all the Edwardian castle towns were established on vacant sites. At Conway a house of the Cistercian order and its associated settlement were removed and at Beaumaris a Welsh community was transplanted to a new location near Rhosfair, a dozen miles away. There were also existing communities at Denbigh and Rhuddlan.

Although Edward established the planned new town of Winchelsea in the South of England, he generally regarded the town as a component in his policy of conquest and pacification. Like his castles, the new towns were an expensive drain on the revenue and labour resources of England and at one stage in the 1280s work was progressing simultaneously on new castle towns at Bere, Caernarvon, Conway, Criccieth and Harlech. In addition to the work at Welsh towns, Edward also invested heavily in strengthening the defences of Berwick-on-Tweed. Although a few of the castle towns of the Middle Ages failed and withered, most endured long after the abandonment of their castles. Today many such places prosper from the tourist trade which their crumbling fortresses attract. But most visitors are so keen to explore the battlements, dungeons and towers that they do not spare a thought for the origins of the settlement nearby.

Castles were also quite frequently associated with monasteries and no less than 170 cases of such an association have been counted. Often the castle founder or his heirs would establish a religious house nearby. There prayers could be said for the souls of the departed members of the castle family and a special burial place for their bodies was provided in the hallowed monastic grounds.

Chapter Eleven

The moat and gatehouse at
Markenfield Hall.

AN ASSORTMENT OF DEFENCES

Castles were not the only forms of defencework which existed. Town walls, fortified manor houses, moated homesteads, fortified bridges and even a few church towers also reflected the insecurities of the age. Of the 249 chartered towns which existed in 1520, no less than 108 were guarded by a circuit of walls. Oxford was unusual in having a double circuit of walls, with the outer ring of walls overlooked by the inner ring in the manner of a concentric castle. Today medieval walls are seldom an obvious feature of the townscape. Often they came to be regarded as a constriction on the development of a town and also as a handy source of masonry which might be pillaged for new building works. In their day, however, town walls were a prominent and costly feature of many town plans, even though their function is still hotly debated. Some scholars regard town walls primarily as declarations of the status of a town, while others stress their practical defensive value. The correct interpretation will vary from case to case. Some town walls, like those of Caernarvon or of Channel ports threatened by French raiding, had a very obvious defensive value, although some others were apparently created as extravagant manifestations of civic pride.

Medieval military engineers did not invent town walls. Several Roman examples existed in England and Wales and at Chester, Lincoln, Winchester and York sections of Roman defensive alignments were included in the medieval circuits. In a sense town walls were out of step with medieval military thinking, which emphasised the private rather than the communal stronghold. The town itself was something of an anachronism in feudal society, an island of relative freedom and opportunity set in a countryside bound by rigid feudal obligations.

Town walls, especially if built to good military standards, were costly, and the longer the urban perimeter which had to be defended, the more costly the wall would be. The cost of walling was recouped, at least in part, by a tax or 'murage grant' which was levied on trade goods coming into the town. Such a toll must have been resented by the traders concerned and may have resulted in a loss of commerce to unwalled trading centres, but at least the town walls will have created a feeling of greater security. Several medieval monarchs encouraged or commanded the building of town walls. In 1215 King John contributed timber for use in the building of walls and turrets at Winchester and York and in the fourteenth century instructions were given for the improvement of the town defences at Gloucester, Canterbury and Winchelsea. The walls of the Edwardian plantation towns of Beaumaris, Caernarvon, Conway, Denbigh and Rhuddlan were all financed by the state. In a few cases defenceworks were incorporated into bridges and examples of fortified bridges can be seen at Monmouth and Warkworth. The bridge across the River Monnow was built around 1272 and about twenty-five years later a fortified gatehouse was added with the gate passage defended by a portcullis and a door, while noxious substances could be dropped on unwelcome visitors via the machicolations above.

York boasts the most celebrated circuit of walls and the history of the city's defences is complex. When York fell to the Danes in 867 a wide palisaded earthbank was cast over the Roman defences and this earthbank was improved and extended in 1068–69 by the Normans, who erected at least five stone gateways. The walls which visitors admire today were built in the middle of the thirteenth century and constructed of fine white limestone imported from Tadcaster. They stand upon the old earthbank of the Viking period and are punctuated by towers added at different times. The oldest are semicircular, then rectangular towers were added and finally the half-hexagonal towers were built. Access to the city was gained via four main gateways or 'bars' which were furnished with portcullises and inner and outer gates. When Scottish raiding posed a threat to the city in the fourteenth century projecting barbicans were added to the gates, although only the barbican of Walmgate Bar survives. In 1511 gunports were inserted on the third-floor level of each gatehouse and each received a pair of cannon. Access to the city by river was controlled by 'boom towers' on either bank, from which chains could be slung across the water. The boom tower known as the Lendal Tower still survives.

Less well known, but in their way no less impressive, are the defences of Tenby on the south coast of Wales. The Normans gained control of the area early in the twelfth century and a keep was built at Tenby, though in the course of time the defences of the town became stronger than the castle that they guarded. A town wall of stone was built around Tenby in the thirteenth century and it was strengthened in 1457 and again in 1588. Other town walls which once were impressive have since been lost. For example, during the reign of Richard II (1377–99) Hull was fortified with walls studded with thirteen towers, all the buildings being accomplished in brick.

The fortified bridge at Monmouth.

The barbican at Walmgate Bar in York.

At Tenby and at York, where the walls are between 6 and 9 feet (1.8 and 2.7m) thick, the town walls constituted viable defences. Some other town walls were much less substantial, leaving room for doubt about whether the shoddy building standards reflected a skimping of work by the townspeople responsible or whether the purpose of the walls was mainly to advertise the status of the town. At Southampton, for example, the quality of much of the work was poor, though the armorial bearings of the town were prominently displayed on the Bargate. Most of the urban defensive architecture of the final stages of the Middle Ages seems to be designed to impress the visitor rather than to depress an attacker. The surviving gateway known as the North Bar at Beverley in Yorkshire was built in locally made bricks in 1409. The elaborate brickwork is still impressive but the work is more a monument to civic pride than to defence. With its large windows, thin walls and hollow buttresses the South Gate which still endures at King's Lynn is another late medieval example of civic showmanship.

Irrespective of their defensive functions – which will have been valued highly in places exposed to Welsh or Scottish invasion or cross-Channel raiding by the French – town walls did offer certain advantages. The encircling of a town with a wall breached by only a limited number of gates or bars made it much simpler for the officials to collect the tolls associated with market trading. At the same time any successful town was likely to expand beyond its armoured girdle of walls and the inhabitants of the extramural neighbourhoods will have enjoyed less security than those living inside the walls. Fortunately for the urban populations of England assaults on towns were much less common than was the case on the Continent. Had they taken place, extramural suburbs would have been plundered and levelled to clear fields of fire, while populations behind the town walls would have endured starvation, disease and possibly pillage and butchery. Regarding the Wars of the Roses, Philippe de Commynes, a French chronicler, wrote that:

> the realm of England enjoys one favour above all other realms that neither the countryside nor the people are destroyed, nor are buildings burnt or demolished. Misfortune falls on soldiers and on nobles . . .

Amongst the most modest of defenceworks are the ditches or moats which so often surrounded the manors of lesser knights and the farmsteads of prosperous yeomen. Moated sites are remarkably numerous; no less than 5300 examples are known and new ones are still being discovered. They come in a wide variety of shapes and sizes; rectangular moats are the most common, but there are also round, semicircular and two-sided and three-sided examples. In some parts of England, especially where there is a heavy clay subsoil to retain surface water, the moated sites are particularly numerous and in a section of the Essex–Hertfordshire border zone 61 sites have been counted in a square of territory with sides 6 miles (10km) in length. Quite frequently dwellings and working farmsteads can still be found standing inside the moated area and in many other cases the traces of former buildings can be recognised.

As with town walls there is a division of expert opinion concerning the question of defence versus status. Those who regard the homestead moats as status symbols argue that the rural worthy

Stokesay Castle, a fortified manor house.

who could not aspire to owning a castle or a fortified manor house would attempt to ape his betters and underline his position in society by having a moat dug around his dwelling. It is certainly true that such moats had no real military value, but those experts who favour a defensive explanation suggest that moats would offer some protection against small bands of brigands or unruly peasants. Both interpretations could be valid and the moat would also have offered other advantages – such as a substantial supply of water available in case of fire.

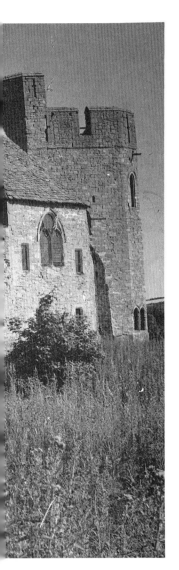

Archaeology has demonstrated that about 44 per cent of excavated moats were created during the period 1200–1325 and that in the remainder of the medieval period the enthusiasm for them declined. Thereafter a few were redeveloped in the course of building imposing moated mansions, but many more were filled in or allowed to silt up. Even so, in many parts of the northern, central and eastern portions of the English lowlands and in parts of Wales which had English landlords the homestead moats are among the most common of the relics of medieval life.

Members of the aristocratic class who were too grand to be satisfied with a moated house yet insufficiently privileged to aspire to a fully developed castle would frequently occupy a fortified manor house. For this they still needed a royal licence to crenellate and the degree of fortification then created could vary considerably. It might involve only the addition of a battlemented tower to an existing house or result in the erection of a scaled-down castle.

Stokesay Castle in Shropshire is one of the finest surviving examples of a fortified medieval manor house. Lawrence of Ludlow, a prosperous wool merchant, obtained a licence to crenellate his home in 1291. He had already modified the old manor house and built the fine open hall which still survives and he crowned the north tower (dating back to around 1240) with a timber-framed upper storey. The fortifications which he added after obtaining his licence to crenellate consisted of a stone tower attached to the south end of the west front of the house and a surrounding moat and curtain wall. These additions did not convert the house into a stronghold of any real substance, but doubtless they enhanced the prestige of their ambitious owner.

Markenfield Hall, near Ripon in Yorkshire, is a well preserved example of a fortified manor house of the early fourteenth century. It lies in an area once vulnerable to far-ranging Scottish raiding and John de Markingfield gained his licence to crenellate in 1310. The stone buildings are arranged around the margins of a rectangular moat and face towards the central courtyard. Movement across the moat was controlled by a drawbridge overlooked by the surviving gatehouse. The defences at Markenfield were probably sufficient to exclude a small raiding party but many of the defensive trappings associated with fortified manors in the more secure regions of England were largely for show. Greys Court, Rotherfield Greys in Oxfordshire, is a good example. The fourteenth-century house was surrounded by a low wall and built into this wall were four small

battlemented towers of flint and brick. As defences they would have proved inadequate, but doubtless they impressed the more welcome visitors.

Longthorpe Tower, near Peterborough, is an unusual fortification. Early in the fourteenth century a massive tower some 40 feet (12m) tall with walls more than 6 feet (c. 2m) thick was added to an undefended mansion. The two lower storeys of the tower were vaulted in stone to eliminate the risk of burning rafters and in some respects the tower resembles a throwback to the Norman keep. The reasons why such a secure refuge was built here are uncertain, although it may have been inspired by fears of French raiders advancing up the River Nene.

In practice the line between the castle and the fortified manor house is not easy to draw. None of the examples given in the preceding paragraphs could seriously be regarded as a castle, even though Stokesay is known as 'Stokesay Castle'. Some writers would regard Bodiam, in Sussex, as a fortified manor, despite the fact that to most visitors it will appear to be the very epitome of the popular perception of the medieval castle. During the fourteenth century private castles were built in considerable numbers. They were not capable of resisting a great host, nor in some cases even a small host. Nevertheless, though their credibility varied, they were not sham castles such as were built in later centuries. We might accept them as 'castles of chivalry', and they are the subject of the chapter which follows.

In a few places medieval church towers were fortified. One of the best examples is Bedale Church in Yorkshire, where the tower staircase was guarded by a portcullis. Fortified church towers were also built in the troubled border country, as at Ancroft and Edlingham in Northumberland. However not all the cases which have been suggested may really have functioned as refuges. Two other kinds of minor stronghold existed in the form of the pele tower and the fortified farmstead, and as these were closely associated with the troubled Anglo-Scottish borders they are described in Chapter 13.

The defended church tower
at Bedale.

Chapter Twelve

The gatehouse at Helmsley.

CASTLES OF CHIVALRY

The castle was a product of its times. Setting aside its important role as a high-status residence, it was designed and adapted to cope with the worst assaults that fate could hurl against its walls – so far as its owner could afford such costly insurance. In 1295 work began on the great Edwardian castle at Beaumaris. In the event the work was never completely finished but few who were alive at the time will have realised that Beaumaris was the last huge and apparently impregnable castle to be built. Castle building did not end with Beaumaris, but the scale of the work and the multiplicity of the defensive systems incorporated in the great Edwardian castles was never to be replicated.

In 1322 the king controlled some 63 royal castles, a number deemed sufficient for the policing and pacification of the realm. Queenborough Castle in Kent's Isle of Sheppey was a late addition to the royal flock which dated from the 1360s. It was built to guard against French raiding in the Thames estuary and although now lost, it appears to have been constructed to an unusual circular design around a central courtyard with six tall wall towers, two of which bracketed the entrance.

The construction of the great Edwardian castles in Wales was accompanied by a surge in aristocratic enthusiasm for chivalry and heraldry. Both were born in the rough and tumble of the battlefield and both became increasingly elaborate and stylised. Heraldry arose from the need for heavily armoured knights to recognise each other on the field of battle and by the thirteenth century the distinctive arms of a warrior had become hereditary. After a favourable marriage was made it came to be customary for the heiress to link the arms of her family with those of her husband and so shields were 'quartered' to include both arms. This led to the development of arms so complicated that they periodically had to be revised and simplified. Meanwhile the possession of arms became a crucial symbol of nobility and family arms were flaunted on liveries, walls, woodwork and fabrics. As a result the king's heralds were given the task of arbitrating on arms and the right to bear them.

The word 'chivalry' derives from a French word for a mounted warrior and was almost synonymous with knighthood. While the medieval knight and noble could, and often did, behave in a beastly manner he liked to perceive himself in the most favourable light. He recognised three classes in society: the churchmen who tended the souls of the community; the labourers and artisans who produced material goods; and the warriors, who protected all Christian souls from their enemies. In battle warriors who shared a code of honour enjoyed an advantage over less steadfast adversaries but during the early medieval centuries the pursuit of war for its own sake led to widespread destruction and disruption. The Church responded to this challenge by adding a moral dimension to the code of loyalty and thus distinguishing between just and unjust causes. The marriage of Christian principles to the ancient code of warriors marked the beginning of the ritual of chivalry and the romance of knighthood. The movement affected the whole of the Western civilised world, so that knights could consider themselves to be members of an international order of nobility. The experiences of the crusades strengthened the bonds of knighthood and the growth in the popularity of tournaments helped to glamourise it. A new and important dimension was added with the growth of the romantic cult of courtly love. Old legends were revamped to accord with the principles of chivalry and none was more popular than those concerning King Arthur and the Order of the Round Table.

In these ways the medieval nobles created a glamorous world which they could inhabit, even though their real actions all too often fell far short of those required by the code of chivalry, which, nevertheless, did offer some practical advantages. The emphasis on the importance of valour and martial prowess made it much harder to evade the call to arms, even though the outcomes of many of the later medieval encounters were settled by mercenaries whose standards of behaviour left a great deal to be desired.

Edward I was both a great commander and a devotee of chivalry and he did much to promote the popularity of the tournament. One was staged on the Lleyn Peninsula during the building of his castles in North Wales. About fifty years later, inspired by the Arthurian legends, Edward III founded the Order of the Garter in 1349 as a celebration of the virtue of the Countess of Salisbury, the target of his exploits in courtly love. During the fourteenth century the romance of chivalry thoroughly permeated and to some extent dominated the values of aristocratic society. People of substance who had fallen under its spell naturally sought to inhabit their own little Camelots and this helped to perpetuate the era of the private castle. The buildings which resulted bore no comparison to places like Beaumaris or Harlech and some were no more than fortified manors. As the castles of chivalry developed they became more ostentatious and agreeable as places in which to live but less capable of withstanding attack. In fact they existed as stepping

The gatehouse at Boarstall.

stones from the robust but spartan castles of the earlier medieval centuries to the great country mansions of the Tudor and Elizabethan eras. In some cases the walls and towers of the new castles were very weak and the most militarily viable portion of the castle was the great gatehouse, as exemplified by Maxstoke in Warwickshire of the 1340s. An impressive gatehouse of 1312 survives at Boarstall in Buckinghamshire and a gatehouse of the 1380s is all that survives of Donnington Castle in Berkshire.

The most popular lay-out was that of the 'quadrangular castle' – a rectangle with towers at the corners and at the mid-points of three of the sides with a large gatehouse in the middle of the fourth side. Where such a form was used the ranges of domestic, garrison and storage accommodation could be set out along the inner faces of the castle walls, with the rooms facing inwards towards the open courtyard. A much more individualistic plan can be seen at Nunney Castle in Somerset. The castle was built in the 1370s by Sir John de la Mare who had campaigned in France and won sufficient booty to finance it. His experiences there must have influenced his choice because he adopted a towered keep design, then popular in France. The core of the castle exists as a rectangular tower four storeys high, with projecting round towers at each corner. It was surrounded by a wet moat and built inside the square bailey of an earlier castle. Water-filled moats were frequently incorporated into the designs of castles of the fourteenth and fifteenth centuries and were associated with modest strongholds, like Boarstall, and more imposing ones, like Bodiam. Many earlier moats were dry, as at White Castle, near Monmouth.

Castles of chivalry were not always the products of romance and several did have a distinct military role to play. Mettingham Castle, in Suffolk, was built in the 1340s by an admiral, John de Norwich, and it was intended that the castle would provide a refuge for the people of the locality in the event of a coastal raid. Bodiam Castle, in Sussex, is one of the most spectacular of the castles of chivalry. It was built by Sir Edward Dallingrigge who obtained his licence to build in 1385 and designed it both as an impressive residence and as a stronghold which would protect the adjacent territory against French raiding on the nearby coast. The licence which Sir Edward received from Richard II empowered him to strengthen the site 'with a wall of stone and lime, and crenellate and construct and make into a castle his manor house of Bodiam, near the sea in the county of Sussex, for defence of the adjacent county and resistance

to our enemies'. The castle was necessary because the English fleet had lost control of the English Channel and the fleets of France and Castile were invading at will.

The gatehouse at Bodiam Castle.

Set within a wide rectangular moat, Bodiam was more strongly and thoughtfully designed than many other castles of its period, although its lay-out was typical of current fashion. It embodied a rectangular plan with four circular angle towers, three rectangular towers in mid-wall positions – one of which formed a postern gate – and a double-towered gatehouse. Provision was made to accommodate a garrison of mercenaries and the domestic suites were organised in such a way that the mercenaries were segregated from the noble family and could, should they prove treacherous, be excluded from three of the angle towers and from the main and subsidiary entrances. The gatehouse was equipped with a portcullis and gates which could close it to members of a mutinous garrison approaching from the courtyard.

Although the mighty endowment of royal castles could have been expected to impose peace upon the realm there were other forces at work which severely undermined stability and periodically resulted in outbreaks of anarchy. They concerned changes in the way that armies and garrisons were recruited. With the growth of a money economy the old feudalism gave way to what has been called 'bastard feudalism'. Previously castles had been lightly manned until trouble arose, and then the feudal levies were conscripted to form the garrison and serve their lord as soldiers. The substitution of money rents for feudal services affected most areas of life and in the fourteenth century gave rise to the recruitment of large permanent forces of mercenaries. The system had originated in 1160 during a campaign by Henry II in Toulouse. Faced by the threat that part of his army would dissolve as his knights completed their forty days of military service, the king developed an idea that knights could commute their obligation for a money payment of 'scutage' or shield money. The money thus collected could then be used to hire professional soldiers. As time went on prosperous vassals of the greater lords would tend to meet their obligations by undertaking to contribute a force of armed men to serve in the private army of the noble concerned. At Bodiam the arms of the celebrated soldier Sir Robert Knollys can be seen carved in stone above the rear gate to the castle. Sir Edward Dallingrigge had served under Sir Robert in the French campaigns and it is likely that Sir Edward had entered into an indenture with his superior and had agreed to contribute a contingent of soldiers to his army.

Private armies grew and multiplied under the custom of 'livery and maintenance'. Professional soldiers in the employ of a particular lord would wear his livery and serve him in his conflicts and adventures in return for their maintenance. So long as the monarch had a firm control of his barons, livery and maintenance facilitated the mustering of a large and professional army, but if royal power lapsed the private armies were likely to be unleashed against each other or against the monarch himself. The practice continued into the fifteenth century; in 1449, for example, one Walter Strickland entered into an indenture with the Earl of Salisbury. He agreed to recruit a force of 290 armed men which he would place at the disposal of the Earl and in return he would enjoy the Earl's protection and receive a yearly salary and a share of the booty captured by the host.

Livery and maintenance seems to have affected castle design in two ways. First, it encouraged the development of strongholds within the castle, like gatehouses or keeps, which the lord and his loyal retainers could hold against a disaffected garrison. Secondly, now that the noble family was not surrounded by friendly vassals but by ruthless hirelings they tended to seek a more separate existence and this encouraged the development of more comfortable private suites of rooms.

No castle of chivalry had the faintest hope of resisting a royal siege and any castle owner would have been out of his mind if he had attempted to provoke such an encounter. However these castles were built during unsettled times and most were capable of coping with the more commonplace threats of the age. Southern castles, like Bodiam, could reasonably expect that no French raiding party would be allowed either the time or resources needed to establish and execute a siege of major proportions. Similarly other quadrangular castles of the period were proof against insurgencies launched by the local peasantry and could also offer some effective resistance to the average private army. Since these mercenary forces frequently achieved their masters' ends through bullying tactics, the possession of a modest stronghold was a distinct asset. Serious attempts to take a castle of chivalry by siege were not particularly common. One did occur at Caister Castle in 1469 when Sir John Paston attempted to hold the castle against the Duke of Norfolk, who had claimed it as his own. In the event the castle fell and its downfall was attributed to shortages of food, gunpowder and morale and to doubts that the besieged would be relieved.

During their campaigns in France the English armies became well versed in siege techniques. There were distinct differences in the strategies employed by the rival armies. Although they enjoyed a superiority in numbers the French tended to exploit their 'home ground' advantage by resorting to the fixed defences of their castles. When they ventured out they trusted to the might of their massed armoured cavalry. In contrast, the English placed their faith in the archers armed with longbows, and at Agincourt this faith was vindicated, quite possibly to the surprise of all concerned. During the Wars of the Roses the opposed forces did not resort to a castle-based strategy but resolved their contest in battles on the open field.

Two fine quadrangular castles were built in Yorkshire. Sherriff Hutton Castle was built by John de Neville in 1382 and although only the two western towers survive it was a palace castle of some standing. Leland wrote of it that 'I saw no house in the North so like a Princely Logginges.' Bolton Castle in Wensleydale is unusually well preserved. Richard le Scrope obtained a licence to crenellate in

*Langley Castle,
Northumberland, a
fourteenth-century tower
house.*

1379 and had already negotiated a contract with a master builder, John Lewyn, concerning the work at Bolton. The contract survives and shows that Lewyn was to provide all the necessary building materials, including timber and lime for the mortar, although Scrope would supply fuel for lime burning and the scaffolding and would meet the cost of transporting materials to the building site. The plan adopted was characteristic of a northern quadrangular castle and it was built around a courtyard measuring 91 feet by 54

feet (28m by 16m) with wall ranges three storeys high and projecting angle towers four and five storeys high with turrets at the
mid-points of the north and south sides. Lewyn was paid 100
shillings for each perch of masonry built, a perch amounting to a
20 feet by 3 feet (6m by 0.9m) section. Although the castle has a
superficially martial appearance it was overlooked by higher
ground and functioned more as a spacious palace than as a stronghold. It staged a stout resistance when garrisoned for Charles I in
1645 but it was not built to resist artillery and the north-west tower,
which received the worst of the Parliamentary artillery bombard-
ment, was weakened and collapsed during a gale in 1761. The castle
was more in its element while serving as a prison for Mary Queen of
Scots in 1568. She had a retinue of forty and the well appointed
castle was able to accommodate her in some style.

Other quadrangular palace castles were built in the north, such as
Lumley in Co. Durham or Wressle, near Selby in Yorkshire. The
smaller northern castles sometimes favoured the alternative design
of the tower house in which all the accommodation was combined
in a rectangular block. Harewood Castle in Yorkshire is a good
example. It was built by William de Alburgh after 1366 with no
internal courtyard and small towers constructed into the corner
angles. The great hall and its adjacent kitchen were at ground-
floor level with a solar and chapel above, while bedchambers and
garderobes were located in the angle towers. Langley Castle in
Northumberland was built to a similar design.

Chapter Thirteen

THE CASTL

*Eilean Donan Castle, Highland, occupies a
small island which was fortified against Viking
raiders in the thirteenth century.*

In many respects the medieval Scottish realm was even less stable than England. The early medieval kings of Scotland adopted feudalism as a means by which they could secure the loyalty of their vassals and thereby strengthen their authority. However, although feudalism could be established in Southern, Central and Eastern Scotland a much more deeply rooted system of clan loyalties persisted in the Highlands, where the clan chieftains were the real monarchs of the glen. When looking north the Scottish kings were reminded of their impotence, while to the south lay England, a powerful neighbour ever likely to exploit the weaknesses of the Scots. Meanwhile the marchlands between the two kingdoms became populated by a warlike society whose exploits could variously bolster or jeopardise the affairs of their kings.

Motte-and-bailey castles were introduced as a means of extending fedual control. When King William the Lion (1165–1214) subdued Ross in 1179 he built a number of mottes, like Redcastle on the Black Isle. Royal castles were built at Inverness and Elgin in stone while feudal nobles also built castles which served as the administrative headquarters of their estates, like the castle of the Comyn dynasty at Castle Roy in Abernethy.

In the Norman period the Anglo-Scottish border was disputed. Cumbria lay outside Norman control until Carlisle was captured and rebuilt in 1092, and it still remained a battleground. In 1237 both sides agreed upon the border between the two kingdoms, though in 1296 Edward I pressed his claim to the overlordship of Scotland. Although his invasion failed to secure his grip upon the kingdom it did achieve the annexation of Berwick. In the Borders a mixed population developed with a northern or lowland Scots dialect of English becoming established by the time of Edward's invasion. The people of the Borders were periodically disunited by war, but (like those of modern Ireland) they also had much in common. Sometimes disputes were resolved at Border meeting places like Norham.

English adventurism combined with fears of Scottish links with France undermined the stability achieved by the frontier agreement of 1237. Edward's invasion of 1296 stirred a cauldron of violence and bitterness which ravaged the Borders and during the reign of Edward's weak successor Scottish forces raided deep into Yorkshire following their victory at Bannockburn in 1314. In the ensuing chaos Border dynasties emerged and exerted despotic powers. The Percys became Earls of Northumberland in 1377 and the Nevilles, Earls of Westmorland in 1398. The heads of these families were made Wardens of the Scottish March, and with the support of royal armies they prevented a 'back-door' invasion of England while the main English forces were campaigning in France. On the other side of the border the mighty Douglas dynasty wielded comparable powers. At the close of the fourteenth century the Earls of Douglas held greater power than the weak Stewart kings. The sixth Earl is said to have never ridden abroad without a retinue of at least a thousand armed retainers. These men, reputed to have been mustered from the ranks of thieves and murderers, were recruited by indentures known as bonds of manrent, the Scottish equivalent of the English custom of livery and mainte-nance. They were known as 'jackmen' on account of their jacks or armoured leather jerkins.

Feuding between the rival earls led to raids which devastated the Border region and threatened to undermine the peace of the entire realm. Richard II sought to avoid the dangerous union of his Border barons by fuelling a feud between the Percys and Nevilles and he introduced magnates like John of Gaunt to serve as royal lieute-nants in the North. The troubled centuries spawned a host of castles great and small and created conditions in which lesser gentry, farmers and even priests sought solace by fortifying their homes.

The main stronghold of the Douglas dynasty was Tantallon castle, built around 1370 on a rocky promontory jutting into the Firth of Forth. The promontory was guarded by a rock-cut ditch and the great screen of the curtain wall. A round tower was built at either end of the curtain and in its middle there was a square gatehouse with accommodation for the earl. Inside the curtain wall were domestic buildings, one containing a mess hall for the jack-men at ground-floor level and with a great hall for the lord placed above it. Earl Douglas had fought on the French side at Poitiers and his castle of Tantallon was a product of this age. Though more than a mere castle of chivalry, with its high curtain and gatehouse it did present a very imposing face to the visitor, but later it had to be modified to cope with new developments in artillery. The Douglas Earl known as 'Archibald the Grim' built the great rectangular tower of Threave Castle on an island in the River Dee near Castle Douglas around 1380. It stood five storeys tall and had walls some 8 feet (2.4m) thick. The entrance was at second-floor level and was reached by removable steps. This tower was built neither for show nor for comfort but echoed the spartan solidity of a Norman keep. Archibald the Grim also rebuilt Bothwell Castle, which occupies a promontory formed by a sharp loop of the River Clyde.

The relationship between the Douglases and the Scottish monarchs varied from the extremes of loyalty and disaffection and bullying. Royal castles of the Scottish kings stood at Edinburgh and Stirling and both castles were substantially altered during the fourteenth century. Edinburgh Castle enjoys a superb defensive site, standing on a volcanic hill which presents a sheer face to the east; the winding approach path was barred by gates and exposed to fire from above. Of the fortifications which survive, the oldest portions are the east curtain wall and tower basement, belonging to the fourteenth century. In 1989 excavations at Edinburgh Castle produced a bone comb of the eighth to tenth century AD. This evidence of Dark Age occupation supports the idea that the castle rock was the site of the ancient stronghold of Din Eidyn. The tribesmen of Din Eidyn were slain in a battle at Catterick by the Angles, according to the Dark Age Celtic poem, the 'Gododdin'. Stirling Castle also exploited a steep-sided hill and the two baileys of the castle were approached by a wide causeway. Near Stirling is Doune Castle, built towards the end of the fourteenth century by Robert Stewart who served as Regent of Scotland during the eighteen-year captivity in England of James I (1406–37) of Scotland. An unusual plan was adopted which was tailored to the advantages provided by the site which occupies a peninsula between two rivers. This allowed the might of fortifications to be concentrated in the landward frontage of the castle where the lord of the castle was able to control the defence from his command post in the gate-house. As in some other castles of the fourteenth century separate halls were provided for the lord and his liveried retainers.

Dunnottar Castle, near Stonehaven, occupies another spectacu-lar site upon a cliff bastion washed by the grey waters of the North Sea. The oldest of the surviving defences date from the fourteenth century and, as at Tantallon and Doune, they guard the landward approaches. A curtain wall was built across the entrance causeway and a keep was constructed to exploit the natural advantage of a rock called 'the Fiddlehead' which commanded the causeway. Any attackers who breached the door and portcullis of the gateway in the curtain were then obliged to scale a steep flight of steps to the Fiddlehead. In 1652 Dunnottar was the only castle retained in Royalist hands and the Scottish crown and sceptre were brought here for safe keeping. Although the castle fell to Cromwell's troops after a siege which lasted for eight months the regalia were smuggled away.

As Tantallon was to the Douglases, so Warkworth Castle was to their frequent enemies, the Percies. The castle occupies a bluff inside a loop of the River Coquet and began as a motte-and-bailey which had both stone and timber defences at the time of its capture by the Scots in 1173. Then a stone keep was developed upon the motte and a curtain wall around the bailey. At various times during the twelfth, thirteenth and early fourteenth centuries the defences were strengthened. In 1332 the Barony of Warkworth passed to the Percy family and in 1377 Henry Percy became the first Earl of Northumberland, responsible for defending the north-eastern approaches to England against Scottish invasions. After acquiring their new title and responsibilities the Percies built a great tower house here to supersede the original keep, which has now vanished. The tower house had the unusual lay-out of a central block about 75 feet (23m) square with wings projecting from the mid-point of each side. The ground-floor level, containing storerooms, guardrooms and a prison, had walls some 10 feet (3m) thick and the two storeys above contained domestic accommodation on a scale to match the new-found dignity of the dynasty.

The Percy family controlled another great Northumbrian castle at Alnwick. This probably originated as a motte-and-bailey castle built by Gilbert de Tyson, the Conqueror's standard-bearer at Hastings. In due course Alnwick acquired a stone shell keep and curtain walls around the two baileys flanking the keep. In 1309 Henry de Percy bought the castle and in the years that followed it was developed as one of the key frontier strongholds. Seven towers were added to the shell wall and work was done on the gatehouses. Henry's son was responsible for the immensely strong outer gatehouse. In the eighteenth and nineteenth centuries the castle experienced heavy restoration but it still preserves much of its commanding medieval presence.

Bamburgh was another Northumbrian stronghold which experienced heavy Victorian restoration. Its history of fortification is an extremely long one. Bamburgh was a Dark Age capital and the site was occupied in Roman times. In the twelfth century a keep was built on the coastal rocky ridge and at the beginning of the thirteenth century the castle was extended so that its three baileys commanded the whole of the cliff-faced ridge. Additions to strengthen the royal castle were made throughout the century. Dunstanburgh Castle, standing on tall cliffs overlooking the North Sea, had a shorter history, being built in 1313 for the second Earl of Lancaster, enlarged by John of Gaunt in the fourteenth century, taken by the Yorkists in the Wars of the Roses and slighted. Norham Castle was built by the Bishop of Durham in 1121 and taken by the Scots in 1136. When Henry II regained control of Northumbria in 1157 Norham was one of the Border castles which he rebuilt in stone. The keep is unusually tall, being raised from three to five storeys early in the fifteenth century. It rises to a height of 90 feet (27m). The keep and castle were heavily damaged when besieged by James IV of Scotland in 1513.

The bloody medieval history of the Border country is engraved on the landscape and the culture of the region. The outlook of the times is preserved in the Scottish ballard 'Lammastide' which tells how 'the doughty Douglas' launched a raid on England at harvest time. He invited the Gordons, Grahams and Lindsays to join him, and later the Gordons rued their refusal to take part in the pillage. Raiding around Newcastle and 'Bamburghshire' Douglas left three towers blazing on Redesdale fell before riding up to the walls of a castle and challenging Lord Percy to personal combat:

> Then up and spake proud Percy then
> And oh! but he spake high
> Saying, 'I am laird o' this castle
> My wife is a lady gay.'
> 'If thou art laird o' this castle
> Sae weel it pleases me
> For e'er I cross the border fell
> The ain o' us shall die.'

Needless to add, Douglas speared Lord Percy, leaving his widow to mourn from the battlements.

Violent feuding of this kind was not confined to the Borders, and a not dissimilar Scottish ballad recalls a typical Highland raid in which the lord of Inverey advanced down Deeside in North-East Scotland to steal the cattle of the Baron of Brackley. When the host arrived at Brackley's gates only the baron, his wife and his brother were present to man the defences. Choosing death rather than dishonour, Brackley went out to fight alone, and after he was slain his evil wife entertained his murderers. But in the last verse of the ballad the seal is set on the feud:

There's grief in the kitchen
But there's mirth in the hall
For the baron o'Brackley
Is deed and awa'
Then up spake his young son
Frae his nurse's knee
'Oh when I grow to be a man
It's avenged I'll be'.

In the Border region the almost incessant raiding and lawlessness obliged people of quite modest social standing to fortify their homes in the later medieval centuries. In this way a distinctive collection of defences evolved. At their grandest these defence-works could result in fortifications comparable with those of fortified manors in the south. Aydon Castle, near Hexham in Northumberland, is an example. Here the license to crenellate was obtained in 1305, and the need for defence became obvious. In 1312 the Scots burned Hexham and nearby Corbridge and in 1314 they achieved their famous victory at Bannockburn. Robert de Raymes, the owner of Aydon, wrote in 1315 that he had 'lately fortified his dwelling at Aydon with a wall of stone and lime against the king's enemies, the Scots'. The wall that he referred to had a square and a round flanking tower and guarded the three sides of the house which were not protected by the steep bank of the Aydon Burn.

In 1544 the English wardens of the marches reported to Henry VIII on the effects of recent forays into the shires of Berwick and Roxburgh. They had cast down or burned 192 villages, towers, farmsteads, fortified houses and parish churches, killed 403 Scots and taken 816 Scottish prisoners as well as 10,386 cattle and 12,492 sheep. The Scottish government was well aware of the destruction and losses which resulted from such forays and in 1535 the Scottish Parliament had passed an Act which required that

. . . every landed man dwelling on or near the border having land worth £100 a year shall build a 'barmkin' upon his land in a place most convenient and of stone and lime. The area of the barmkin should be three score square feet and the wall should be one ell thick [34.5 inches; 87.6cm] and six ells high and it should be used by the tenants and their goods in times of strife. If he wishes, the owner can build a tower within the barmkin for his own safety.

The barmkin was a sort of miniature bailey, an open space surrounded by a strong and lofty wall where people and their livestock could seek shelter while raids were in progress. A barmkin could be freestanding, but generally it was associated with a fortified residence of some kind. Most have perished but an example survives at Burneside Hall, in Cumbria. The peculiar word 'barmkin' may be a corruption of barbican, which refers to an outer gateway.

Most of the minor fortifications of the northern marchlands date from the troubled period between the invasion of Scotland by Edward I and the union of the English and Scottish crowns in 1603. Many of them are known as 'pele towers': rectangular towers which can be freestanding or attached to a residence and which sometimes stood within a barmkin. They vary very considerably in their size and form, so that the largest might almost be classed as castles. Generally they were built three storeys tall and were battlemented. The bottom level was used for storage and the upper two floors were residential, so that in many respects the pele tower represented a miniaturised throwback to the old Norman keeps. Similarly, peles standing in barmkins were reminiscent of old keep and bailey castles. However, one must treat the terminology with care, for in medieval times the term 'pele' was apparently applied to positions strongly fortified with earth and timber defences. A survey of 1541 describes refuges built in Tynedale as peles although they bear no resemblance to the current understanding of the term:

> . . . they are built in naturally strong positions and consist of walls and roofs of squared oak trees bound together and morticed. The whole is covered with earth and turves so that they may not be set on fire and they are so strong that only with great force and numbers could they be cast down.

The situation is confused even further by a Scottish description of 1578 which identifies 'pailes' as pyramidical towers built of earth alone. The word is thought to derive from the Latin *palus*, a stake.

The best-known pele tower is the Vicar's Pele which stands by the roadside in the churchyard at Corbridge. It was built in the early years of the fourteenth century to afford refuge to the parish priest. It is a freestanding rectangular tower of three storeys and its entrance is blocked by an iron-armoured door at ground-floor level. This floor was used for storage, the floor above contained a living room and the third floor was a bedroom. It is hard to imagine that any priest would wish to be entombed alone in such a building while Scottish raiders prowled just outside. However the machicolations on the parapet and the provision of wooden shutters to close the embrasures suggest that in times of trouble the pele tower would be actively defended by a body of men. Chipchase Tower, beside the North Tyne, is a much more substantial rectangular tower which dates from about 1340. It stands four storeys tall and small turrets rise from the corners. It is attached to a residential wing from which access to the tower was gained at first-floor level.

At least 58 pele towers can still be identified in Cumbria alone, and one of the best examples is attached to the domestic accommodation at Sizergh Castle. It too was built around 1340 and served as a refuge for the Strickland family. Although the pele towers are clustered along both sides of the Anglo-Scottish border a few were built in places which were only vulnerable to deeply penetrating invasions. Nappa Hall in Wensleydale is a fine example, built by the old campaigner Thomas Metcalfe around 1460. Here a domestic range is sandwiched between two towers, the defensible west tower and the lower east tower, which contained the kitchen and service rooms.

The Border wars gave rise to a number of confusing terms, and another example is 'bastle'. It derives from a French word for a temporary camp or defensive out-work and was applied to a fortified residence somewhere between the status of a tower and a pele, although today it is used to describe the defended farmsteads of the frontier region. Bastles seem to date mainly from the period 1550–1650 and housed livestock on the lower level with domestic accommodation above. Their walls were around 4 feet (1.2m) thick and drawbars guarded the doors while entrance to the upper level was normally via a ladder which could be pulled up. The bastle was a standardised form of building measuring about 36 feet (11m) by 20 feet (6m) and bastles were concentrated in a Border zone of about 20 miles (32km) wide.

Chapter Fourteen

THE

Carew Castle, Dyfed,
contains substantial remains
of the Edwardian period.

CASTLE IN WALES AND IRELAND

When King Offa had his great Dyke built in the eighth century to mark the western bounds of his Mercian kingdom he was, to some extent, recognising his inability to conquer the independent Welsh territories. The medieval kings of England launched a sequence of invasions in their attempts to repeat the mastery over Wales which the Romans had achieved long ago. Before the medieval period had run its course these attempts proved successful. In the meantime, however, the principality had acquired a great legacy of castles, some built by invaders and others by Welsh nobles.

In 1063 Harold Godwinson achieved a virtual conquest of Wales and brought the head of a Welsh prince and the figurehead from his ship to the court of Edward the Confessor. From the Norman Conquest, at the dawn of the age of castle building, Wales existed as a territory ripe for conquest and as a battleground where warriors could prove their prowess without disturbing the peace of the English kingdom. By 1100 the manors strung out along the border zone had acquired an English or a Welsh identity, though Welsh was spoken in various Shropshire parishes which now have no identity crisis. Bases such as Chester, Oswestry, Shrewsbury, Gloucester and Hereford served as assembly points for invasions and forays into Wales. In 1093 the great Welsh prince Rhys ap Twedwr was slain in a Norman ambush and it appeared that the Norman conquest of Wales would be as easy as that of England. In the event, however, the terrain greatly favoured the resistance fighters. Although invasion routes facilitated the subjugation of the southern strip, the rough terrain and narrow valleys of the interior were made for guerrilla raids and ambushes and enabled the Welsh to fight or run as they chose. Even the elements seemed to conspire against the invaders and in 1165 a great invasion launched from Oswestry by Henry II was abandoned in the Berwyn Mountains on account of torrential rain and flooding. In 1402 an invasion by Henry IV (1399–1413) met a similar fate.

The piecemeal colonisation of Wales was more successful, with warriors from the English Midlands extending their estates westwards and establishing feudal manors on the receding frontiers of Welsh culture and control. The introduction of English peasant tenants and burgesses and the involvement of Welsh people in the activities of plantation towns all helped to secure the more accessible territories under English control. The Anglo-Norman lords of the Welsh Marches enjoyed more independence of action than

*The circular keep of
Longtown Castle.*

those in the English heartlands and a law of the march developed which had both English and Welsh features. As on the Scottish Borders, various places were recognised as centres for the arbitration of disputes, which occurred on 'love-days'.

The marcher lords, however, were not always united in their purposes and the free Welsh princes proved adept at exploiting any divisions which arose between them. Llywelyn ap Gruffyd, Prince of Gwynedd, (1246–82), emerged as a great leader, although in 1247 he and his brother were forced to accept a humiliating treaty imposed by Henry III. A decade later England was divided and Llywelyn sided with the baronial opposition led by Simon de Montfort. The tables were now reversed, and in 1267 a new treaty confirmed Llywelyn in his conquests and gave him mastery over most of Wales, with the title of Prince of Wales.

Wales, however, was not united but divided between the rival principalities of Gwynedd, Powys and Deheubarth. When the English invaded again in 1277 they arrived as the supporters of Powys against its powerful neighbour Gwynedd. Division also occurred within dynasties, and Llywelyn had one of his brothers imprisoned for twenty-two years. As the power of Gwynedd was consolidated, so the emergent Welsh state loomed as a growing threat to English interests. Much of the country was already in the hands of English marcher lords, whose territories formed a buffer zone between the independent Welsh territories and the English heartlands. It was a fear of an expansionist Gwynedd which led to the building of the great castle at Caerphilly. Great marcher lords, like the Bohuns of Herefordshire and Brecon, the Clares of Gloucestershire and Glamorgan and the Mortimers of Chirk, lent their forces to the support of Edward I and this led to the crushing of Welsh resistance at the end of the thirteenth century and the defeat was sealed by the building of the great Edwardian castles.

After the English invasion of 1277 Llywelyn emerged as prince in little more than title. Great English castles were raised at Aberystwyth, Flint, Rhuddlan and Builth. In 1282 Llywelyn's brother, Dafydd, launched an attack on Hawarden Castle and sparked a new uprising. The Llywelyn forces took the castles at Flint and Rhuddlan and advanced towards Chester and a new English invasion was mounted. Llywelyn was heading north from his base at Aberedw Castle when he was captured and slain by an English force, while Dafydd was captured and hung, drawn and quartered at Shrewsbury in 1283. Now the second group of Edwardian castles

was begun at Caernarvon, Harlech, Conway and Beaumaris to throttle the mountainous heartland of Welsh resistance.

In 1400 Owen Glendower was proclaimed Prince of Wales and this coincided with a rising mood of nationalism among the Welsh. He seized the castles at Aberystwyth, Criccieth and Harlech and suddenly Wales was again aflame. Divisions in the English nobility were exploited, a French fleet dominated the Irish Sea and a French and Welsh army advanced as far as Worcester. Gradually, however, the revolt lost its impetus and the castles which had fallen were recaptured one by one. By 1410 Glendower was defeated and he went into hiding. Eventually a lasting peace was obtained after Henry Tudor, a descendant of Glendower, landed at Milford Haven in 1485 and marched eastwards from Pembroke Castle. His defeat of Richard III at Bosworth Field united the thrones of England and Wales under a monarch acceptable to both nations.

The keep of around 1150 surrounded by the walls and towers of the later castle of Goodrich.

Castles appeared in the Welsh Marches before the Norman Conquest, with several mottes being cast up here by Norman favourites of Edward the Confessor. At Ewas Harold, in the Black Mountains, one can still see the great castle mound built by Lord Osbern. Edward's nephew, Ralph, built a castle at Hereford and Richards Castle, to the south of Ludlow, is thought to be another pre-Conquest motte. For the year 1051 the Anglo-Saxon Chronicle records that:

> The foreigners had built a castle in Herefordshire in Earl Sweyne's territory and inflicted all injuries and insults they could upon the king's men in that region.

After their conquest of England the Normans embarked upon the colonisation of Wales with all their characteristic vigour. However, although perhaps encouraged at first by their conquests in the other Celtic territory of Brittany, they soon discovered that victories in the field were followed by guerrilla fighting and insurgencies. Faced with a number of setbacks, the Normans developed a new system of administration and control. The old towns of Chester, Hereford and Shrewsbury became the foci of semi-independent earldoms. Meanwhile the old divisions of conquered Welsh territory re-emerged as 'marcher lordships'. They numbered 153 in total and each existed as an almost autonomous kingdom within the Norman orbit. Most of these lordships were dominated by a castle and frequently plantation towns were developed beside the castle. While Welsh law survived in the independent lands, in the pacified marches a separate 'custom of the march' was applied. In this way the marches existed as a buffer zone between the free Welsh and the English territories in which the rule of the king was absolute. In return for securing difficult territories the marcher lords enjoyed virtual autonomy. They controlled and administered justice and exercised other privileges, like the designation of hunting forests and the collection of fines, which were royal monopolies else-where.

These privileges depended upon the ability of each lord to secure his own territory and consequently castles assumed a heightened importance within the marches. As a result of the latitude allowed to their owners, these castles frequently existed as the bases for robber barons who terrorised the surrounding countryside. Order-icus Vitalis described them as being 'puffed up with pride' and wrote that:

. . . they shielded their men at arms who most outrageously
robbed the people and ravished the women and those only
incurred their wrath who were driven by these grievous fronts
to be allowed in their remonstrances.

At the end of the eleventh century the Normans extended their
dominion across South Wales. The control of the coastal lands was
considered a necessary prelude to the invasion of Ireland. Pembrokeshire developed as a bastion of Anglo-Norman control and an
earth and timber stronghold was established at Pembroke in 1097.
In the north the Norman castle at Rhuddlan served as a forward
outpost of the earldom of Chester and in the centre of the marches
the castle at Hen Domen operated as a frontier post of the Earl of
Shrewsbury and as a base for an attack mounted on Cardigan.

During the early medieval centuries the Welsh Marches acquired
a greater density of strongholds than could be found in any other
British province. The borderlands of Gwent were guarded by a trio
of fortresses: Grosmont, Skenfrith and White Castle. They were
charged with the task of guarding the Golden Valley, maintaining
the Norman presence in Abergavenny and blocking the Welsh
invasion route to the English lowlands. Grosmont Castle was
probably first fortified in the years following the Norman Conquest
of England, though the visible remains are of a keep-like hall block
of the early thirteenth century guarded by round towers and a
gatehouse added later in that century. Henry III came to Grosmont
to secure the loyalty of his border lords during the uprising led by
Llywelyn the Great, but was forced to leave in haste when Llywelyn
launched a surprise attack and captured the castle. Skenfrith originated as a motte-and-bailey castle of the early twelfth century and
the site is dominated by the round keep of the early thirteenth
century surrounded by a four-sided curtain wall with four of the
original five towers still standing. White Castle is so named because
of the whitened plaster which once covered its masonry. A timber
castle was erected here around 1100 and a square stone keep was
added in the middle of the century. In the 1180s a curtain wall was
added to the bailey and in the second half of the next century the
defences were redeveloped. The keep was dismantled and the
curtain was extended across its remains and armoured with six
round towers, two of which formed a gatehouse.

Altogether at least eighty castles were built in the south of Wales
during the medieval period. They include the thirteenth-century
castles like Cilgerran, Llawhaden, Llanstephan and Manorbier and

*The walls and towers of
Grosmont Castle.*

Edwardian castles like Carew, Kidwelly and Caerphilly. Earlier notions of fortification are exemplified by the round keeps at Bronllys, Caldicot, Castell Coch and Tretower.

The instability of life in the troubled borderlands encouraged men of the middle rank who would not otherwise have aspired to fortifications to build defences against petty banditry. Moated sites are associated with areas in the south and east of Wales and, where records survive, they are found to have been built mainly by settlers with English names. Such men will have feared both the consequences of Welsh uprisings and the depredations of the private armies of the marcher lords.

Castle building was not confined to the Norman and English invaders, for the Welsh leaders imitated the strongholds of their adversaries. Welsh interest in castle building appears to date from the start of the twelfth century. In 1111 a Welsh leader was exploring a possible castle site near Welshpool when he was assassinated and in 1116 a Welsh castle was built at Cymmer in the old county of Merioneth. Although the terrain of upland Wales was the key to Welsh defensive strategy, castles were still valued, as much if not more for their use in Welsh dynastic struggles as for bastions against English attacks. However, castles were never as numerous in the free Welsh territories as they were in the occupied marches, where each lord had a stronghold where vassals from surrounding manors might shelter during a Welsh raid or uprising. Dolwyddelan Castle near Betwys-y-Coed was the birthplace of Llywelyn the Great (1194–1240), who joined the English barons in revolt against King John in 1215 and secured a recognition of Welsh rights in Magna Carta. The castle was built by Llywelyn's father around 1170, it fell to Edward I in 1282 and now only a rectangular tower of the thirteenth century remains. Criccieth Castle was built about the year 1200 as a rectangular keep within a triangular curtain wall. It was taken by Edward I in his campaign of 1282–83 and an English castle was built inside the Welsh one. Its strength was concentrated in a twin-towered gatehouse, which still commands the ruins of its predecessor.

Dolbadarn Castle, between Caernarvon and Dolwyddelan, was another Welsh castle which fell into English hands during Edward's invasion of 1282–83. The first castle to be built here consisted of a triangular curtain wall which enclosed the summit of a rocky knoll. Early in the thirteenth century a circular keep of three storeys was added, almost certainly at the command of Llywelyn the Great. After the castle was captured for Edward I by the Earl of Pembroke its timbers were removed for use in the royal castle at Caernarvon and Dolbadarn was never again fortified. A fourth Welsh castle in Gwynedd was Castell y Bere, built for Llywelyn the Great in 1221. It was a keep and bailey castle with the bailey built to a triangular plan with round towers at each corner. It was destroyed by Edward I in 1294.

The great Edwardian programme of castle building appeared to suffocate all Welsh hopes of independence until the peace of the realm was shattered by the Glendower uprising. Glendower directed his first blow at Ruthin Castle, near Denbigh. The castle was held by Lord Grey who had attempted to rob Glendower of his inheritance. The castle town of Ruthin was set aflame but Ruthin Castle held. Two years later, however, Glendower defeated an English army at Vyrnwy and his old adversary was captured and ransomed for the sum of 10,000 marks. In 1403 Henry IV ordered the owners of twenty-two castles in South Wales to supply and fortify their strongholds – a sure sign that the castle in Wales still enjoyed some military currency. But by the end of the century many of these castles were ruined and abandoned.

The last true private medieval castle to be built in Britain was Raglan Castle, near Pontypool. Although the date of the castle is controversial, the site of an earlier castle appears to have been refortified by the Yorkist supporter Sir William ap Thomas after about 1435 or by his son, William, after 1469. Large parts of the fifteenth-century work survive. The walled enclosure is divided into two courts by a great hall set across its middle but the site was dominated by the great 'Yellow Tower of Gwent', surrounded by a wide wet moat. Five storeys tall and hexagonal in plan, it was furnished both with arrow slits and with gunports. The castle appears to have been designed to operate in the age of artillery and provision was made both for the defensive use of guns and for the use of angled masonry to deflect incoming missiles. The reasons for building such a magnificent late addition to the castle flock are not known. Possibly the Glendower revolt was still producing ripples of uncertainty but the design adopted, with the great keep dominating the approaches to the less resilient residence, echoed current Continental thinking.

In Ireland the defensive tradition appears to have begun with the defended farmsteads or 'raths', where a central area contained a farmstead and was surrounded by one or more circuits of banks and ditches and breached by an entrance causeway. Between 30,000 and 40,000 of these raths can still be identified and in any flight across Ireland many can be recognised patterning the fieldscape like fairy rings. Raths had an amazingly long history. They were built and occupied from Neolithic until medieval times. Hillforts, in contrast, had a much shorter currency. They did not become numerous until the period of the Roman occupation of Southern Britain and are a characteristic of the early historical rather than of the prehistoric period. Certain of the larger hillforts, Dun Ailinne, Downpatrick, Clogher, Navan and Tara, were ceremonial places, the sites of royal palaces and the initiation of kings. In addition to these complicated ceremonial sites, where ritual celebrations took place in distant times, there are about 200 other forts in Ireland which have a single circuit of bank and ditch – a modest total considering that Britain has more than 20,000 hillforts. Ireland also contains only about fifty examples of multivallate forts, those with more than one circuit of ramparts, and these are concentrated in the west of the country. Moghane, in Co. Clare, is the largest example and covers an area of 27 acres (11ha). The most spectacular of the ancient defenceworks of Ireland are the stone walled forts or 'cashels' of the rocky countryside of the west. These are elaborate translations of the earthen rath into stone, and in consequence many examples are well preserved. Most of the examples studied date not from the prehistoric period but to the centuries known in Britain as the Dark Ages. Unlike the earthen raths, the cashels often had chambers constructed into the thicknesses of their walls. These walls were built of gathered rubble, usually limestone, which was laid in irregular courses of drystone walling. Sometimes a 'chevaux-de-frise' of upright angular blocks of stone guarded the approaches to a cashel. A fine example of this can be seen at Dun Aengus cashel on the Aran Islands and other notable cashels on Inishmore include Dun Oghil and Dun Onaght; Caher Conor on Inishmaan is another fine example.

The conquest of Southern Wales secured a Norman routeway for expansion into Ireland and in 1170 the Normans landed at Dublin. Within three decades they had conquered a great deal of the eastern part of the island and warriors secured the conquered territories with motte-and-bailey castles. Around 1200 they began to build stone castles in Ireland and more than forty castles built by Norman colonists during the thirteenth century still survive. Some of these castles formed the nuclei for urban growth and the new castle towns were sometimes defended by town walls.

The most notable of the Norman castles in Ireland is at Trim, overlooking the River Boyne. In *The Song of Dermot and the Earl* there is a description of the original castle built here by the Norman conqueror, Hugh de Lacy:

> Then Hugh de Lacy
> Fortified a house at Trim
> And threw a ditch around it
> And then enclosed it with a palisade
> Within the house he then placed
> Brave knights of great worth.

Excavations carried out at Trim Castle in the 1970s uncovered the ditch which had surrounded Hugh de Lacy's timber keep. This keep was demolished in 1212 and work on the stone castle began. It was built tall and square with walls 12 feet (3.5m) thick and small rectangular towers projected from the midpoints. In 1210 King John had confiscated the de Lacy fortifications when he visited Trim; he returned them in 1215 and the castle which survives was completed in 1220. In 1241 the de Lacy estate passed to the de Greville family and it was about this time that the stone keep was surrounded by a D-shaped curtain wall which enclosed the bailey, with the straight limb of the D running beside the river. The keep itself was made more secure by heaping a plinth of earth over the foot of the walls to frustrate any attempts to undermine them.

An Irish castle which appears much as it did in the late Middle Ages can be explored at Bunratty, quite close to Shannon Airport. The castle was built by Sioda MacConmara in the mid-fifteenth century on what was then an island in the Shannon River, and by the end of the century it had become the seat of the O'Briens, the Kings of Thomond.

The castle is entered via a drawbridge leading to a small lobby which has a 'murder hole' overhead through which scalding water or oil could be poured on unwelcome intruders. Beyond the lobby is the main guard, a large chamber where retainers and the garrison were accommodated and which also served as the general dining room of the castle, a line marked on the floor dividing the space allocated for the nobility and officers from the area used by the common soldiery and servants. Dungeons and storerooms also occupied the ground-floor level.

On the floor above is the great hall of the kings (and later earls) of

Thomond. It is 16 feet (4.8m) high, 16 feet (4.8m) long and 10 feet (3m) wide and was used as a state and banqueting room, the high table and the seat of state of the earl standing on a raised dais. There is a small kitchen adjacent but food for larger gatherings must have been prepared in an outbuilding. A public chapel occupied the south-east tower of the great hall and the earls had their private chapel on the floor above.

The private accommodation for the noble family was situated over the great hall and comprised two solars, the earl's bedroom and pantry, a bedroom for guests and a room for the chaplain. Efforts have been made to restore the castle interior to the way in which it appeared around 400 years ago and so Bunratty Castle is particularly evocative of the heyday of the Irish castle.

The castles built in Ireland during the earlier medieval centuries were the strongholds of the Anglo-Norman conquerors, but during the fifteenth century the native Irish leaders began to build their own fortifications to resist attacks by both the foreign lords and their own countrymen. Most of those built were variations on the theme of the tower house, so popular in Scotland and the Anglo-Scottish border country. It is estimated that in the period between 1150 and 1600 around 3000 castles and tower houses were built in Ireland.

Chapter Fifteen

The fortified manor house known as Hever Castle.

THE ROAD TO REDUNDANCY

In Scotland, Ireland and on the Continent, the castle survived the passing of the Middle Ages, but in England and Wales castles had effectively been discarded well before the end of the medieval period. They were not completely obsolete as strongholds and many were garrisoned and subsequently battered and dismantled in the course of the Civil War. In the meantime, however, political life and military thinking had gravitated away from the costly art of castle building even if the sham castle was still enjoying much favour as a setting for aristocratic life.

During the fifteenth century no royal castles were built and few licences to crenellate were granted – as compared to the previous century, for which the historian M. W. Thompson has counted 380 licences. Several explanations have been offered for the decline of the castle but the reasons are various and it must be remembered that a castle itself produced virtually no wealth but was a continual source of outlay on repairs and maintenance. If this drain on the wealth of the castle owner was to be tolerated the castle needed a real reason for its existence. Otherwise an alternative and more fashionable form of residence would have to be explored.

The most commonly offered explanation for the decline of the castle concerns its supposed vulnerability to 'the gunpowder revolution'. The origins of the cannon are uncertain but a chronicler describing the rebellion of the Duke of Gloucester in 1267 mentioned the advance on London by the army of Henry III, which was 'making daily assaults when guns and other ordnance were shot into the city'. The nature of the artillery concerned here is not specified and it is not until 1326 that there is a definite mention of brass cannon firing iron balls being used by the defenders of Florence. In 1340 the city of Lille is known to have paid for 'three tubes of thunder and 100 arrows'. In due course early brass or bronze cannon firing arrows were superseded by more formidable weapons, and cannon of forged iron are known to have been made at Caen in 1375. Before a more effective use could be made of artillery it was necessary to improve the manufacture of gunpowder, a blend of saltpeter, sulphur and charcoal. These ingredients had tended to separate when gunpowder was stored or transported, but early in the fifteenth century the technique of 'corning' powder was developed in France. The constituents were mixed together in a wet paste which was allowed to dry to form a cake and the cake was then crumbled to make granules of stable gunpowder. The new formulation provided a much more rapid ignition and was three times as effective as the old gunpowder had been. Towards the end of the fourteenth century more efficient gun carriages were developed, allowing for the faster deployment of guns, although this was more significant in mobile battles than in siege warfare.

The first response of the castle builders to the arrival of gun-powder on the battlefield was to provide gunloops which allowed artillery to be mounted in a castle. Such an early response is evident in the gatehouse of Bodiam Castle of the 1390s, where the walls are pierced by gunports set a few feet above ground level. Around twenty gunports of an inverted keyhole shape were included in the west gate of Canterbury, built in 1375–81. Such innovations were confined to southern castles which were threatened by French raiders, and this suggests that artillery still did not have a signi-ficant role to play in domestic conflicts. However, in contrast to developments on the Continent, English castles were not modified in ways that would provide greater protection against the use of the new artillery by their attackers. By the 1520s the use of cast iron ammunition allowed artillery to inflict serious damage on castle masonry and on the Continent this led to the thickening of some walls and the lowering of some towers, which then served as gun platforms. In England the effect of artillery improvement was confined to making provision for guns to be mounted in castles – as at Raglan – but nothing was done to improve the resistance of castles to artillery used by attackers. When mounted in castles the new artillery weapons could be used to destroy the traditional siege engines of the attackers, so rather than destroying castles the artillery appears to have contributed to their defence. Early siege artillery seems to have constituted as great a threat to those who fired it as to those who were fired upon, and in 1460 James II of Scotland (1437–60) was killed when a gun known as 'The Lion' exploded at the siege of Roxburgh.

On the whole it appears that gunpowder was not the primary cause of the demise of the castle. At the time when castles were still playing a leading military role the cannons which might be ranged against them were too primitive to constitute a serious threat. As artillery improved castles could have been strengthened in ways that would have allowed them to offer a credible resistance. The fact that such remedies were not applied suggests that the castle had already fallen from favour as a prime strategic weapon. This had already taken place by the time that the Tudor monarchs exercised a monopoly on the casting of great guns and the use of gunpowder.

The economic problems which eroded the ability of many lords to contemplate a heavy investment in the building of castles became severe in the fourteenth century. The Pestilence or Black Death made its first great assault in 1348 and recurred at frequent intervals throughout the remainder of the Middle Ages. When it first struck, Britain was an over-populated land and a deteriorating climate had intensified the problems of supporting an over-blown population on the diminishing agricultural resources. Labour was cheap and over-abundant. However, after the Pestilence had extinguished between a third and a half of the population labour became both scarce and expensive and there was not only a shortage of masons and artisans to engage in castle works, but also of peasants to produce the wealth to finance them. Some castle owners were more fortunate than others. The Greys at Ruthin combined prudent management of their estates with several carefully considered marriages and also preserved the male line, while Lord Hebert at Raglan sought a more active involvement in commerce than was common amongst the aristocratic families. But during the fifteenth century there was a great fluctuation in the fortunes of the noble dynasties and this led to the concentration of wealth and titles in some families and the relative impoverishment of others. Lucrative royal service and perceptive decisions in choosing whether to support the Yorkist or Lancastrian cause could make a significant difference. William Herbert of Raglan supported Edward IV at the battle of Mortimer's Cross in 1461 and won great royal favour and profit, though his partisanship in supporting the Yorkist cause also obliged him to invest heavily in castle works.

Even if a family retained the wherewithal to build or improve their castle they still needed to man its walls and under Henry VII (1485–1509) the practice of livery and maintenance was outlawed. Henry was strong and secure enough to impose this Act of Parliament whereas the 1327 statute against maintenance and the 1377 one against livery had been flouted by the barons. Francis Bacon described how Henry reacted when confronted by the liveried retainers of the Earl of Oxford at Castle Hedingham:

> The King called the Earl to him and said, 'My Lord, I have heard much of your hospitality, but I see it is greater than the speech. These handsome gentlemen and yeomen, which I see on both sides of me, are sure your menial servants.' The Earl

smiled, and said, 'It may please your Grace that they were not for mine call. They are most of them my retainers that are come to do me service at such a time as this, and chiefly to your Grace.' The King started a little, and said, 'By my faith, my Lord, I thank you for your good cheer, but I may not endure to have my law broken in my sight. My attorney must speak with you.' And it is part of the report that the Earl compounded for no less than 15,000 marks.

Henry VII and his Tudor dynasty had emerged victorious from the Wars of the Roses which had seen the wholesale slaughter of members of the baronial class. He was in a position of strength which allowed him to curtail the power of the nobility in ways which his predecessors would have envied. The newfound might of the monarchy was not only evident in the power, if needed, to recruit great armies of mercenaries which no rival could match, but also in the strict control over castle building. In fact, Henry sought to avoid involvement with Parliament so far as was possible. He achieved this by avoiding war and by raising revenue through swingeing taxes on the nobility – a policy which further reduced their military ambitions and encouraged some to recoup their losses through commerce. The last private castle of any substance was begun at Thornbury in Gloucestershire in 1511 to an ambitious and ornate courtyard plan. This was to be the fortified abode of the third Edward Stafford, Duke of Buckingham. In 1521, however, Henry VIII learned of rumours that the duke was stockpiling armaments and recruiting a private army in Wales. The duke was arrested and beheaded and his castle was never completed. It combined practical defences and a forecourt, where a private army could muster, with ornate bow windows and ornamental brick chimneys belonging more to the stately home than to a castle. A licence to crenellate and also to found a college of canons had actually been given, but what resulted was a hybrid mansion-castle.

The castle was both a home and a fortress and if a member of the castle-dwelling class was to abandon tradition then he needed an alternative abode which would still enhance rather than demean his status. In fact, unfortified mansions had always existed. They ranged from the splendour of royal palaces like Westminster or Woodstock to the manor houses which a lord would visit in the course of his perambulations around his estates. From the four-teenth century the alternative existed in the form of the unfortified or lightly fortified courtyard house with its ranges of rooms arranged around one or more enclosed courtyards.

Some experts believe that the courtyard castle provided the mould from which the courtyard house was cast, but the case is not proven. The arrangement of buildings around courtyards had been a feature of monastic sites which were centuries older than the first courtyard houses and was also adopted at the university colleges. It might also be argued that the lay-out developed spontaneously from the growth of medieval houses, fuelled by ever-increasing demands for more private suites of rooms and more accommodation for servants. Such houses tended to sprout new building ranges at right angles to the original hall block, so that L-, H- and E-shaped lay-outs developed. Eventually it might have been considered more convenient and agreeable to arrange the ranges around a rectangular courtyard. However, such a plan was only practical where the house concerned accommodated a family of real substance, a family that needed to offer dwelling spaces for a considerable number of officials, retainers and servants. Such accommodation could be provided in cellular dwelling units which were set side-by-side in a long building range – a lay-out which was difficult to reconcile in a castle plan where the various towers would interfere with the arrangement.

For an unfortified courtyard lay-out to be adopted the owner would need to be convinced that it was acceptable for families of quality to dispense with the traditional castle-centered lifestyle and that status could survive without the trappings of nobility provided by fortifications of the more serious kind. The building during the fifteenth century of unfortified courtyard palaces by bishops at places like Southwell in Nottinghamshire and Knole in Kent may have helped to establish the acceptability of the new form. At More, near Rickmansworth, a license to crenellate was awarded in 1426, but excavation has shown that what resulted was essentially a courtyard house of brick. Cotehele in Cornwall contains elements of an earlier fortified house but it is essentially a well-preserved example of the home of a prosperous squire of the last stages of the Middle Ages. Haddon Hall in Derbyshire contains work from all centuries from the twelfth to the seventeenth but it basically consists of a courtyard house of the fourteenth century with a lower court added in the fifteenth century. Houses such as these with ranges of cellular rooms were designed for life resembling that lived by students in halls of residence. The officials, retainers, visitors and functionaries accommodated would gather to dine in the great hall of the courtyard house and then disperse to their self-contained lodging rooms.

A study of the abandonment of castles at the end of the Middle Ages has been made by M. W. Thompson. He shows that in the descriptions of journeys by the chronicler Leland in 1535–45 the conditions of 258 castles are mentioned. Of these, 91 were still in normal use, 30 were partially derelict and 137 were ruinous. The days of the castle were past, although people still had difficulty in adjusting to the fact and still perceived the castle as the focus and symbol of lordship. After all, it had played these roles for a very long time and its successor, the stately home, had still to establish an identity. Uncertainties about such matters still encouraged the digging of moats and the building of battlements, but these were sham defences which secured only the status of the family within.

Chapter Sixteen

At the time when the castle was declining in England fortified towers were proliferating in the less secure lands of the North; between the fourteenth and the seventeenth centuries some 270 examples were built in the Borders region alone and many more were built in the central and Highland regions of Scotland and in Ireland. It is debatable whether these tower houses indicate the direction in which castle building might have evolved in England, for in the unsettled northern areas the need to fortify was imposed upon families of moderate means who would, had they lived elsewhere, have occupied open manor houses.

In England there was some movement in the direction of building strongly fortified towers. Faced with the possibility of attacks not only from the enemy without but also from a disaffected garrison, the owners of castles of livery and maintenance had concentrated strength in great gatehouses. In this way they sought to control the entrance to their castles and simultaneously retain the occupation of a viable and self-contained stronghold which might be held against the enemy within. Gatehouses, however, were not made for domestic convenience. They were breached by entrances and housed defensive paraphernalia in the forms of doors, portcullises and gear for raising the drawbridge. Much more convenient accommodation might be enjoyed in a tower of great strength. At Warkworth Castle a great tower house was built around 1385 on a mound facing the gatehouse from across the bailey. It existed as an independent fortified residence that was comparable in role to the gatehouse of some earlier castles.

One of the most extravagant executions of the tower house concept was Tattershall Castle, in Lincolnshire. The first castle here was built around 1250 but its modest ruins are completely dominated by the great brick tower house built by the High Treasurer of England, Lord Cromwell, in the years 1432–46. Cromwell built his castle as a rectangular tower some 120 feet (37m) in height and with boldly projecting angle towers at the four corners. Above the sunken basement there were four storeys in the main body of the tower, while the angle towers, which rise above the tower, had six floor levels. Each floor level accommodated one large room, the staircase was contained in one of the angle towers and smaller rooms were contained in the three remaining towers. Tattershall Castle did not, however, exist as a self-contained tower house as did the tower at Warkworth, for its kitchen, buttery, pantry and chapel were housed in a directly adjacent building which has since

The spectacular tower house of Castle Fraser, built around 1600.

190

THE TOWERS OF THE NORTH

been lost. Rather than being an independent fortress, the Tattershall tower was an extremely strong addition to the pre-existing castle on the site which was probably partly demolished to make way for the new shrine to chivalry.

Though resembling Tattershall in many respects, Nunney Castle, in Somerset, was a genuine tower house and a more serious fortification. Built in stone rather than brick it was the creation of John de la Mare, a veteran of the French wars. When he built his castle in the years after 1373 Sir John was surely influenced by the forms of castle which were popular in France. The tower stood within the rectangular bailey of an earlier castle and was surrounded by a wet moat. It was rectangular in form, 80 feet (24m) long by 40 feet (12m) wide with boldly projecting round towers about 30 feet (9m) in diameter at the four corner angles. It stood four storeys tall and each storey contained a main chamber with smaller rooms in each of the angle towers. Above the level of the machicolations each tower narrowed and was originally crowned by a conical roof, which must have emphasised Nunney's resemblance to a French château.

The great tower house at Ashby de la Zouch Castle, in Leicestershire, was a similar exposition of the tower house concept, though built a century after Nunney Castle. It was an addition to the existing manor house and in 1474 Lord Hastings surrounded the house with a high curtain wall and built his tower house in the middle of the south front of the wall. The tower was roughly square in plan and originally rose to a height of 90 feet (27m). It contained four storeys and octagonal turrets projected out from the upper two storeys. Clifford's Tower, standing upon an old Norman motte at York, was built to a much different quatrefoil plan, (like a four-leafed clover) but had some of the features of a tower house.

Two of the finest tower houses in the North of England are Chipchase and Belsay, both built in the first half of the fourteenth century and both possibly the work of the same designer. Both also display the oversailing turrets which were to become a feature of Scottish tower house architecture. One of the earliest applications of the tower house concept occurred at Dudley in the West Midlands during the first two decades of the fourteenth century. This was the castle of Sir John de Somery, whose private army terrorised the surrounding countryside. Though the remains are incomplete it seems that this early tower house was only two storeys tall, oblong in plan and with round towers at the angles. It provided Sir John with a hall and kitchen accommodation and a strong base which could be defended in the event of mutiny by the mercenaries housed in the bailey below.

The historical events described in the preceding chapter curtailed the development of the fortified tower house in England, but in Scotland tower houses enjoyed a remarkable popularity and they continued to be built and to evolve until long after the close of the Middle Ages. One of the reasons for the popularity of the design was that it could be modified to suit most pockets. The tower house could be a stark and spartan little tower or it could be a quite imposing stronghold with ample accommodation provided in attached wings.

The popularity of the tower house form in Scotland may also relate to a widespread shortage in that country of constructional timber. As early as 1437, Aeneas Silvius, who was to become Pope Pius II, remarked that the Scots were so destitute of timber that they were obliged to burn stones instead. In a tower house the ground floor rooms and the hall could be vaulted in stone and the vertical emphasis of the building meant that relatively short spans of beams were needed which could serve to support both the floors of the room above and the ceiling of the room beneath. Also, since the rooms were arranged in a vertical stack only one roof with its set of roofing timbers was needed to cover the whole. Stone, in contrast, was available in abundance, allowing the construction of very thick walls with narrow slit-like windows. The towers, with their economical groundplans, did not require vast numbers of retainers to man the battlements but could allow a modest force to stage a credible defence. In these ways tower houses offered security and the trappings of status at a cost which appealed to the thriftiest of owners.

The tower house design could easily be enlarged to provide additional domestic accommodation. This was often done by building an extra wing to produce an L-shaped plan. Such an extension could actually strengthen the tower, for an entrance placed in the hollow angle of the L was flanked on two sides. Sometimes an entrance situated at first- or second-floor level in a freestanding tower was relocated at ground-floor level when the new wing was built. Such L-plan towers became very popular in Scotland in the sixteenth century; Greenknowe Tower near Berwick, of 1581, is a good example. Less frequently two wings or a residential wing and a turret to house a staircase were attached to opposite corners of a tower house, and this arrangement produced a Z-shaped plan. Such a plan was adopted in Huntly Castle, built around 1452, and similar lay-outs can be seen at Claypotts Castle, near Dundee, of 1569, and the ruined Glenbuchat Castle, in Upper Donside, of 1590. Frequently barmkins of the kind described in Chapter 13 were attached to Scottish tower houses, though often they have been removed. A good example survives at Tolquhon Castle, near Aberdeen.

In the typical tower house the ancillary buildings, the brew-house, stillroom, bakehouse, stables and storerooms would be arranged around the courtyard or barmkin. The ground floor of the tower would house the kitchens, from which food was taken up to the communal dining area of the great hall, vaulted in stone, on the first floor. Here the lord would sit at high table and survey his guests and household, just as Norman lords had done centuries before. From the vicinity of the high table a staircase led up to the private suite of the noble family on the floor above, while at the lower end of the hall another staircase gave access to the lord's business room or estate office, also situated at second-floor level. The third floor typically accommodated the lord's picture gallery and the household chapel.

Like the castles of England, the Scottish tower houses evolved into status symbols where the gentility and good taste of the owners could be proclaimed. Under the weak Stewart kings the tower house often had to serve as a stronghold and as a local court of justice, but after the union of the crowns it was able to evolve in the direction of the country mansion. Two extracts from a letter of advice written in 1632 are quoted by Schomberg Scott. One concerns the use of a corner turret:

> Of it you may make a fine cabinet for books and papers, which is so necessary that it cannot be wanting for a man that understands these things and what it is to keep anything from the eyes and fingers of others.

The second is even more telling:

> By any means do not take away the battlement, as some gave me counsel to do so . . . for that is the grace of the house and makes it look like a castle and so noblest.

One of the largest and most splendid of the Scottish tower houses is Castle Fraser, near Aberdeen. It was built at the end of the sixteenth

Sham fortifications and stone cannons at Crathes Castle.

century and followed the typical tower house plan. The great hall occupied the whole of the first-floor level, while extra private accommodation was provided in the square and circular towers attached to opposite corners of the main building. At the start of the seventeenth century the building was embellished with blind machicolations and corner turrets carried through the two uppermost floors, with decorative mouldings and batteries of cannon carved from stone sprouting from above the false machicolations to emphasise the fairytale grandeur.

Crathes Castle, also near Aberdeen, was built in the second half of the sixteenth century for the Burnett family on a south-facing site overlooking the River Dee. Again a heavy emphasis was placed on the decorative effect of crenellation, corbelling and machicolation, with stone cannon again being thrown in for good measure. The original Scottish baronial reached its climax with the completion of another tower house in North-East Scotland, Craigievar Castle, which was finished in 1616.

In these three castles the stern dictates of defence had given way to fanciful decorative gestures but there were scores of slightly older tower houses which quite closely resembled the stone keep towers of the Normans. So close was the resemblance that it might almost seem as though evolution had followed a circular course.

Tower houses also enjoyed great popularity in Ireland. Most Irish counties contain at least fifty examples and in the south-west of Ireland the counties have between 200 and 400 tower houses each. In the counties lying within the English pale a subsidy of £10 was made available early in the fifteenth century to encourage members of the alien nobility to build tower houses, providing that the towers built were more than 40 feet (12m) in height. Meanwhile Irish leaders in the west, where feuds and cattle raids were endemic, built their own tower houses. When Presbyterian settlers were planted in Ireland in the seventeenth century they introduced tower house designs based on Scottish prototypes. Monea Castle in Co. Fermanagh is an example, with out-corbelled round towers reminiscent of those at Castle Fraser.

Dunguaire Castle in Co. Galway is one of the best preserved of the Irish tower houses and is a typical fortified chieftain's dwelling of the sixteenth century. It stands within a six-sided 'bawn' or barmkin on a rocky outcrop beside Kinvarra Bay. Ross Castle in Co. Kerry is a huge fifteenth-century tower enclosed by a bawn with rounded turrets. According to an old prophecy the tower could

only be taken by an attack from across the waters of Lough Leane –
so when Cromwellian troops attacked this Royalist stronghold by
boat the defenders showed a fine regard for legend and surrendered. The earliest datable Irish tower house may be Kilcleif Castle
in Co. Down. It was built early in the fifteenth century as the
residence of the Bishop of Down and may have served as the model
for various later towers.

Chapter Seventeen

On the Continent and in Scotland, castles of substance and grandeur were built in the sixteenth century. In England, in contrast, members of the nobility were exploring new ways of living and developing residences in which the patterns of domestic life were not shaped by the lay-out of curtains and towers. At the same time they did not want to lower their guards too far. At some future date their homes might have to be defended and one also had to be sure that the residence would enhance rather than diminish one's status. With these thoughts in mind various features which were closely associated with aristocratic life – like moats, battlements, machicolations and gatehouses – were generally incorporated into the new arrangements. Other features, like massive stone walls and slit-like windows, imposed such restrictions on domestic convenience that they were gladly abandoned. The degree to which a house was a sham castle or endowed with credible defences varied from place to place but none of the new residences was built with defence as the overriding priority.

The Wars of the Roses involved set-piece battles in open country. Sometimes these battles were precipitated when one army unexpectedly stumbled upon another, but the motives of war were well defined. The combatants fought to capture the government of the country and the taking or holding of territory was now a much lesser consideration. Since castles existed to secure territory they became minor sideshows in the confrontations and could be ignored or bypassed in the ebb and flow of mobile warfare. The only fullscale siege of a private castle was that of the Lancastrian castle at Alnwick in 1461–62, and this castle fell. Neither side was prepared to go to the enormous length of reducing strong castles by siege. Castle design had been perfected by the end of the thirteenth century and this very perfection may have played a part in their decline. If siege warfare imposed an intolerable burden on an attacking force then it was more practical to avoid castles rather than to attempt to conquer them.

In more purposeful castles there had been a tendency for the gatehouse to surrender its primacy in the defensive arrangements to a keep-like tower, as described in the preceding chapter. However, the gatehouse commanded the approaches to the house and was the part of the residence most likely to make a striking impression on the visitor. Oxburgh Hall, in Norfolk, was begun in 1482 and built to a fashionable rectangular courtyard plan and surrounded by a wet rectangular moat. It is dominated by a great gatehouse

The gatehouse at Herstmonceux Castle.

CASTLES OF SHAM AND SHOW

which still stands much as it did when newly built. It consists of a central tower containing the gateway which is flanked by two deeply projecting octagonal towers. The whole house is a wonderful exposition of the craft of Tudor builders in brick but the tops of the towers are embellished with double-stepped embattlements in stone and with false machicolations. The gatehouse embodies many of the old symbols of authority, but had it been built in the pure interests of defence rather than ostentation it would have presented a very different appearance. As though to mock the martial pretensions the walls in the tower overlooking the gateway are breached by the great four-light mullioned window of the 'King's Room', with the three-light window of the 'Queen's Room' just above it. Norfolk was an unruly place in the fifteenth century and the moat surrounding Oxburgh Hall had more than an ornamental value. While probably able to keep a rabble at bay the defences at Oxburgh would scarcely have impressed to any organised force which contained a component of artillery. Like most other buildings, Oxburgh Hall is a product of its political and social environment. The labour supply was still reduced by the ravages of the Black Death and farming was often unprofitable. Soldiers were returning after the close of the Hundred Years War and could be encountered roaming the countryside in marauding bands. In such times members of the upper classes felt a need for houses which could be held against a disorderly rabble or a hostile neighbour even if they were ill-equipped to withstand an organised siege. In the words of historian Dr Saltmarsh, 'Oxburgh represents an enormous investment in personal safety'.

Like many great houses which would follow, Oxburgh was built in brick. It lies in a part of the country which is deprived of good building stone, and without the availability of brick the builders would have been obliged to resort to the use of flints gathered from the fields or have contemplated a less grandiose design in expensive imported stone. The Romans had made extensive use of narrow bricks, which can be seen, for example, coursed with flint in the shore fort of Burgh Castle. The art of brickmaking was revived in the fourteenth century and red brick became highly fashionable in the great houses and show castles of the Tudor era, when the bright, russet hue of brickwork will have provided a striking contrast to the sombre, muted tones of stone. In the middle of the fifteenth century stone was still incorporated in brick palaces for the door and window surrounds, tracery and carved details, but by the

(Opposite above)
Oxburgh Hall

(Opposite below)
Sherborne Old Castle, victim of severe slighting during the Civil War.

(Overleaf)
The moated manor house at Kentwell in Suffolk.

close of the century brick was used throughout and embellishments in ground or moulded brick provided many a flamboyant flourish.

Herstmonceux Castle, in Sussex, predated Oxburgh by forty years and was fifty years younger than Bodiam. In terms of the lay-out of the defences Herstmonceux echoes the Bodiam plan, based on a courtyard lay-out with angle towers and a gatehouse surrounded by a formidable moat. In other respects, however, Herstmonceux was much closer to Oxburgh. The castle was built in brick with four lofty octagonal towers at the angles and with three semi-octagonal towers on each of three sides and two semi-octagonal towers and a great gatehouse on the south front. The gatehouse draws the eye, just as it was intended to do, and is flanked by towers which are semi-octagonal to the height of the three-storey central tower and then rise above the first tier of battlements as semicircular towers. The gatehouse towers are machicolated and pierced for use both by bowmen and gunners, although the brickwork of the central tower is breached by three large windows. In 1936 the historian Hugh Braun wrote:

> At Herstmonceux we can detect the last desperate effort of the wealthy landowners of the south who had been reading too much Malory and were determined to live in castles as in the days of Chivalry. It has brick walls – lofty, but very thin – many slender turrets, a glorious moat reflecting spacious mullioned windows and cross-cut arrow slits lighting the turrets in the great gatehouse. From Herstmonceux we may pass on to Cowdray at Midhurst in the same county where the beautiful Elizabethan manor house keeps its turreted gatehouse but gives up the struggle to be a castle – content with the glories of mullioned windows gazing over green turf and pleasant gardens.

The builder of Herstmonceux was Sir Roger Fiennes and like so many of the castle builders of the time he was a veteran of the French wars. Others included Sir John Fastolf, who built Caister, Ralph, Lord Cromwell, who fortified Tattershall and South Wingfield manor in Derbyshire, Ralph Boteler, who built Sudeley Castle in Gloucestershire, and Sir Andrew Ogard, who built Rye in Hertfordshire. Plunder and booty helped to fund the castle-building projects. The extent to which they were influenced by French castle designs has been disputed, particularly in the case of Herstmonceux, and buildings like this castle or Oxburgh could

(Opposite)
The brick-built great tower at Caister Castle.

have been influenced by smaller fortified and moated manor houses, like John, Lord Cobham's Hever Castle in Kent, or Michael de la Pole, the Earl of Suffolk's Wingfield in Suffolk, built in the closing years of the fourteenth century. Hever demonstrates the fashion for concentrating defences at the front gate approaches to a fortified house. A double moat was provided but three sides of the building were poorly defended. The main frontage was furnished with two little turrets providing flanking fire to the powerful gatehouse.

Sir John Fastolf had fought at Agincourt and campaigned in France until the 1430s. Work at Caister began in 1432 and the castle took more than a decade to complete. It consisted of a rectangular moated enclosure containing a brick courtyard castle with square towers at three corners and a narrow but lofty tower at the north-west angle. This tower was some 90 feet (27m) tall and contained a single hexagonal chamber in each of its five levels and was served by an octagonal stair turret. Both tower and turret were furnished with gunports for artillery. To the north-east of this moated enclosure was a large forecourt surrounded on three sides by a curtain wall which had round towers at its three angles. The fourth unwalled side of the forecourt faced towards the castle proper and was linked by a bridge across the moat to the castle gatehouse. Another forecourt to the west had access by canal to the River Bure and the canal was used to import materials and provisions. A squat round tower, known as the 'barge Tower', may have served as a 'bastille' or advance fortification guarding the approaches to the castle. The design of the castle is unique in Britain and has been compared to a *Wasserburg* or 'water-castle' of the Rhineland – although there is no evidence that Sir John had any German connections. The early history of Caister reveals that the need for serviceable defences had not yet passed. In 1458 the French sea raiders arrived at the gates following the defection of Burgundy from its alliance with England. After Sir John's death, when the castle fell into the hands of the Paston family, the building was defended in 1469 against the 3000-strong force of the Duke of Norfolk, faced an artillery barrage and eventually fell.

In the fifteenth century feuding was a dangerous pastime. Sir John Fastolf had a long-standing feud with John Heydon, who had acquired a Norfolk estate not far from Caister, at Baconsthorpe, in the north-east of the county. Heydon will have felt a little more secure after building the fortified manor of Baconsthorpe Castle around 1460. It was built in the established quadrangular pattern with a rectangular moated enclosure, with square angle towers and with a residential gatehouse in the centre of the south curtain.

At Herstmonceux a licence to crenellate was applied for and granted in 1441 and both this castle and Caister had some value as defences against French coastal raiding. In general, however, the castles described here had limited military pretensions. They presented an imposing martial face to the world even though their machicolations might be fake and their walls just a couple of feet thick. Most importantly, they were built to impress, and there is no doubt that the towering gatehouses and vivid and costly brickwork fully produced the impression intended. In terms of defence they were not designed to deter an army, least of all a royal army. The builders sought a balance between the degree of fortification which might raise dangerous doubts in the mind of the monarch and those which might deter a marauding band of cut-throats. To err on either side of the proper balance might indeed prove risky.

Several other show castles of the fifteenth century have been destroyed or preserve only fragments of their original fabrics. Ampthill Castle, in Bedfordshire, has gone completely but had a double courtyard lay-out and may have resembled Herstmonceux. Sudeley Castle was demolished in the seventeenth century; it also had an inner and an outer court. Rye was built under a licence to crenellate which was granted in 1143 and now only the gatehouse and moats remains.

In 1447 William, Lord Hastings, obtained a licence to crenellate no less than four houses in Leicestershire. These were Ashby de la Zouch, Bagworth, Kirby Muxloe and Thornton. At Ashby Lord Hastings began work in 1474 on a great tower, which is reminiscent of a Scottish tower house, as an addition to his existing manor house. Work at Kirby Muxloe began in 1480 but was never completed, for the ambitious lord was beheaded on the orders of Richard III in 1483 and all work on the new castle as planned was abandoned. The plan was for a large and showy moated castle of quadrangular design. The remains reveal a rectangular gatehouse with octagonal turrets at each corner and one of the seven intended rectangular wall towers. The castle was built in brick, yet designed to make full use of artillery. The lowest floor level in both the gatehouse and tower was equipped to house heavy cannon and had six and seven gunports respectively. The gateway was intended to be protected by stone machicolations. Evidently Hastings planned to build a residence of considerable grandeur in brick with stone dressings with the architecture conforming to a symmetrical plan. This would also have been a fortress of some substance and well provided with guns, even though little consideration was given to the traversing and fields of fire of the armaments.

Although the castles and fortified manors of the fifteenth century made full use of the decorative possibilities presented by brick, they showed no revolutionary advances in castle design. In their layouts most harked back to the long-established quadrangular plan displayed at Bodiam, which was begun almost a century before Kirby Muxloe.

At Layer Marney Towers in Essex, the direction of development in show castle architecture was carried to its conclusion – and beyond. Building between 1510 and 1525 was sponsored by Henry, Lord Marney, and his successor, John. Their efforts produced an enormous eight-storied gatehouse which was intended to exist as the showpiece of a great and ornate mansion of brick. The work was accomplished purely to impress and although the by now traditional gatehouse form was adopted there were no pretensions to defence. Tiers of windows pierced the brickwork of the octagonal gatehouse towers and two vast mullioned windows looked down upon the gateway. The sham battlements and window mouldings were embellished in terracotta decorations bearing Italian Renaissance motifs. So excessive was the scale of the gatehouse that the remainder of the house never materialised.

Well before Layer Marney Towers was begun, a generation of unfortified mansions had appeared. Compton Wynyates in Warwickshire was begun in the 1480s and was designed for comfort rather than defence. It had a moat, drawbridge and sham battlements but was essentially a product of the peace which followed the Wars of the Roses. In the 1530s William Compton, who had a position at the court of Henry VIII, enlarged his house and entertained the king and Catherine of Aragon here. Doubtless they were impressed by the eye-catching brickwork on the towering chimneys – a new symbol of status which owed nothing to military architecture. In 1644 a party of Parliamentarian troops attacked the house, which did well to hold for just two days before being captured. The Parliamentarians then filled in the moat, but they failed to discover a group of the Royalist wounded who were being tended by the Countess of Northampton in the loft.

The changing values in Tudor England may best be represented by the transformations effected at Kenilworth Castle in the same county. The castle was handed over to the barons by King John as part of the Magna Carta settlement in 1215. At this time it had a great keep tower standing on an earlier motte and John had added a curtain wall and the approaches to the stronghold were barred by a great artificial lake. So secure were the defences that the followers of the rebel baron Simon de Montfort held Kenilworth for nine months against the army of Henry III and only a shortage of food forced their eventual surrender. In Tudor times the Duke of Northumberland forfeited his estates and was executed in 1553 after attempting to manipulate the succession of Lady Jane Grey. In 1558 Elizabeth I (1558–1603) restored the family fortunes and the duke's son, Robert Dudley, became a favourite suitor of the queen. In 1563 the queen made Dudley the Earl of Leicester and gave him Kenilworth. He entertained Elizabeth here on three occasions, built a great gatehouse and converted the old castle into a palatial home with suites of rooms being built to accommodate the largest entourage. It was under the Tudor monarchs that the English nobles discovered the pleasures of gracious living and came to accept that status could flourish without the trappings of war.

Chapter Eighteen

The Baddings Tower at Rye, built around 1250 to resist invaders.

DEFENDING THE NATION

D uring the latter part of the Middle Ages a sense of English national identity began to emerge. Previously such sentiments had scarcely developed and loyalties were based on kinship and locality. While the Roman Church exerted a powerful force for unity across the whole of Christendom, under the feudal system society was divided vertically, into classes, rather than horizontally, into nations. The royal castles of the medieval centuries were not concentrated in the invasion-prone frontiers but distributed around the realm in order to control the king's assets and secure territory against uprisings by ambitious barons. The rise of nationhood was paralleled by the decline of private castles, and when the private castle declined the significance of royal castles was also eroded. If a nation existed, however, it had to be defended and the emergence of the nation state was accompanied by the gradual development of a doctrine of national sovereign territory. Under the Tudors the kingdom was internally pacified and attention turned to the strengthening of its vulnerable invasion shores.

The lessons of the Norman Conquest were never completely forgotten, and in the course of the Middle Ages a number of troublesome raids and invasion scares were experienced. When the English barons rebelled against King John they invited the heir to the French throne, Prince Louis, to invade England with a foreign army. The French landed in Kent and shortly after John brought his army down from the north to face them he had a seizure and died in the October of 1216. His nine-year-old son was crowned as Henry III and the prime cause of the barons' revolt was removed. The baronial party was defeated at Lincoln and the French invasion fleet was repulsed off Dover. In the year after John's death a French mercenary, Eustace the Monk, raised a strong fleet to ferry reinforcements for Prince Louis over from France. It was met by a small English fleet and defeated.

The defence of the Channel largely depended on the Cinque Ports, Hastings, New Romney, Hythe, Sandwich and Dover, to which were added Rye and Winchelsea. In return for concessions in taxation these ports supplied the ships which formed the basis of the English navy. In 1328 the throne of France passed to Philip VI, who encouraged his ships to prey on the vessels engaged in the prosperous wool trade between England and Flanders, and in the spring of 1338 the French fleet landed men at Portsmouth who pillaged and burned the town. In the autumn of that year Southampton met a similar fate. The English retaliated with attacks on

Le Treport and Boulogne. In 1340 Philip raised a fleet of 200 vessels and an army of 20,000 men at the port of Sluys with the intention of conquering Flanders and then mounting an invasion of England. However, the invasion fleet was attacked by the English and Flemish fleets and was routed. Then in 1359 a French army of 3000 men was landed at Winchelsea, the town was burned and the inhabitants massacred. In 1377 Rye, Hastings and Portsmouth were burnt and raids were mounted on Poole and the Isle of Wight; an attack on Southampton was beaten off before the French could reach the harbour. In 1416 the French blockaded Portsmouth and the Isle of Wight and in 1473 the English fleet intercepted a raid on Southampton.

This long history of raids and invasion scares formed the background to the invasion phobia which gripped the country during the reign of Henry VIII. In 1519 Charles V of Spain was elected Emperor and in 1522 Henry joined with him in a war against France. The Emperor had a great victory at the Battle of Pavia in 1525 and Henry then realised that this could give the Emperor ascendancy over Europe. He decided to change sides. The Pope also supported the French cause and in 1527 the Emperor's army sacked Rome. When Henry sought a divorce from Catherine of Aragon so that he could marry Anne Boleyn the Pope, now subject to the Emperor, refused to sanction the divorce. Eventually Henry made his break with the Church of Rome and appointed himself as head of the Church in England. Pope Paul III then sought to unite Europe against England and in 1538 Francis I of France and the Emperor Charles V agreed a ten-year truce, the Truce of Nice, which would pave the way for an invasion of England and restore papal authority in the kingdom.

Henry moved swiftly. Commissioners were appointed to defend the coastline and the English fleet was assembled at Portsmouth. He decided to create a system of anti-invasion defences to guard the harbour and the likely landing-places. The blockhouses and forts which he built were not castles but were designed to make use of the latest developments in artillery.

Earlier in the century improvements were made in refining iron. Henry followed all the developments in gun-making technology very carefully and during the 1530s he established gun foundries in London and the Weald which were supervised by skilled gun-founders from the Continent and which gave a home-based alternative to the use of ordnance imported from the Low Countries. Eventually a practical method of casting cannon in iron was developed. Previously guns had been cast in non-ferrous metals, such as brass, or were light pieces made from bars of metal which were bound together to form a barrel. By the time that Henry embarked on his fort-building programme of 1539–47 guns were available in a standardised range of calibres. There were small 'sakers', firing a 6-pound (2.7kg) shot; culverins firing an 18-pound (8kg) shot; basilisks firing a 25-pound (11kg) shot; and demi-cannon firing a 32-pound (14.5kg) shot. With a range of around a mile, these pieces were much more valuable weapons for coastal defence than the old mortars and bombards which had been used during land-based sieges. The artillery pieces were mounted on wheeled gun-carriages, but although these carriages allowed the weapons to traverse in the horizontal plane they only had a limited vertical elevation.

The effectiveness of artillery had been demonstrated in 1494, when French artillery reduced a whole series of fortresses during the march through Italy of the army of Charles VIII. Both the victorious English and the Scots employed artillery at the Battle of Flodden in 1513. However, conflicting evidence makes it difficult to assess the true potency of artillery fire. The Roundheads, for example, found their guns unable to effect terminal destruction on the medieval castle at Corfe even though they pounded away at the masonry for a period of nine months.

A great variety of coastal defenceworks were built, suggesting that, rather than drawing upon Continental parallels, the military engineers were experimenting with their own ideas. The range included 'bulwarks' or earthworks which have left few traces, simple blockhouses and quite elaborate artillery fortresses.

In 1532 Henry was the author of a plan to modernise the defences of Calais to make them better able to exploit the developments in artillery. The Dublin tower there was to be reduced in height and

> '. . . made broder, and massed up with lyme and stone and thereupon a platfourme to be made to bere a grete pece of ordinaunce, as well to beate over the bulwerke there, as to scoure the contreth thereaboutes.

At Carlisle in 1541 Henry employed a Bohemian engineer, Stephen von Haschenperg, to adapt the medieval keep and curtain wall to house artillery.

Henry's adversaries controlled France, Spain and the Low

Countries and Henry originally intended to fortify the whole southern and eastern coastline from Hull to South Wales. In the event the work was concentrated on the south-eastern shores; the south-western shores already enjoyed a measure of protection. Dartmouth Castle, in Devon, was built by the population of the town with the assistance of Henry VII between 1481 and 1495. Situated on the west bank of the river Dart, it had a strong square tower pierced by seven gunports. Guns covered the estuary although each gun had little facility for traverse or elevation. The gunners would have been obliged to hold their fire until the hostile ships entered the narrow approaches and crossed their sights. Shortly after the completion of Dartmouth several small blockhouses were built to guard the south-western coast.

The artillery forts built by Henry VIII were individually designed but they did tend to share a number of features. When in action the forts would be engaged in artillery duels with ships of the invasion fleet and so they needed to be solidly constructed. They were of a low, compact and squat form with thick walls. In 1941 a German bomb landed on the fort built by Henry at Deal but only succeeded in damaging some later additons to the structure. The main fort had a squat and cylindrical central keep which was surrounded by lower round bastions which were directly attached either to the keep or to a curtain wall which surrounded the keep. Guns were mounted on the summit of the keep and could be moved on their carriages to cover a complete arc. The round bastions might be three, four or six in number; they housed guns on their flat summits and others firing through gunports. The mounting of guns in positions that were open to the sky facilitated the rapid clearing of the heavy clouds of smoke which the gunpowder produced. Where embrasures were used they were widely splayed to provide a generous traverse for the guns. Curving walls were presented in every direction and it was believed that such surfaces would tend to deflect enemy shot. They were sturdy, businesslike strongholds containing none of the decorative flourishes which one might associate with castles of chivalry. The smaller blockhouses also varied in their designs. The one at Edgcumbe, in Cornwall, was square, but most were built to a D-shaped plan.

Each fortress and blockhouse was a component in a defensive strategy designed to deny the French or Spanish invaders access to anchorages and landing places where an army could be set ashore. A threat was posed by clandestine landings which could establish a detachment of soldiers to attack the forts from the landward side. For this reason the castles were built in such a way as to allow their guns to be fired in all directions. They were surrounded by moats, usually dry moats, that could be raked with fire by musketeers or archers positioned on the lower bastions. The moat was spanned by a drawbridge and the entrances accommodated barred doors, portcullises and murder holes borrowed from the design of medieval castles. In times of war a very strong garrison could be housed, though in more settled times the garrison was much smaller – thirty-five men in the case of the fort at Deal in Kent.

Henry's coastal forts incorporated many of the features developed by military engineers on the Continent who were attempting to improve both the defensive and offensive use of strongholds in the age of artillery. However, the forts were original in the way that the concepts were integrated, notably in that bastions were clustered so tightly together around the central cylindrical towers and multiple tiers of artillery platforms were combined. These innovations fused compactness and strength with a remarkable concentration of fire power.

The relative importance of the roles played by Stephen von Haschenperg, Henry's military engineer, and the king in the design of these forts is not known. Stephen is known to have been responsible for the work at Camber fort and Sandgate fort and Henry was said to have been involved in planning the castles at Deal, Walmer and Southsea. It is possible that the king was more than an active and enthusiastic sponsor.

The system began at the Thames estuary with blockhouses on the northern and southern banks of the river at Tilbury and Gravesend which guarded the approaches to the capital. The Downs in Kent provided perhaps the most vulnerable stretches of invasion coast and a trio of closely spaced fortresses at Sandown, Deal and Walmer guarded the coastline between Dover and Sandwich. Dover was provided with a blockhouse to supplement the existing defences, a fourth fortress was built at Sandgate, between Folkestone and Hythe, and a fifth fortress was built at Camber near Rye.

A second concentration of fortresses guarded the Solent and the approaches to Portsmouth and Southampton. Fortresses were built at Southsea, near Portsmouth at the entrance to Spithead and at Calshot on the western flank of Southampton Water. Calshot stood on a shingle spit, as did Hurst fortress which, with another fortress at Yarmouth on the Isle of Wight, guarded the western approaches to the Solent.

Another fortress was built at Sandown on the Isle of Wight and a pair of blockhouses guarded the approaches to Cowes. Further west, a fort on Brownsea Island (built by the townspeople of Poole) guarded the entrance to Poole harbour and the fort at Sandsfoot, on Portland Bill, was supplemented by a blockhouse built near Weymouth. The entrance to Carrick Roads at Falmouth was guarded by two fortresses, St Mawes to the east and Pendennis to the west. Following the king's visit to Hull in 1540 a castle linked to two blockhouses was built there and blockhouses were also built at Harwich. Semicircular casements for artillery were also built around the Tower of London.

Much of the revenue needed to create the new system of coastal defence was derived from finance accrued from the dissolution of the monasteries and the sale of monastic properties. The records show that a small blockhouse cost around £500, while an artillery fort would cost in the region of £5000. The castles and bulwarks in Kent which defended the Downs cost some £27,000. Each gunner was paid the modest sum of 6d (2.6 new pence) a day and was obliged to provide his own handgun. For comparison, this pay fell between the levels paid to skilled artisans and labourers.

Camber fortress was unusual in that it originated as a circular blockhouse built early in Henry's reign in 1512–14. Under the close guidance of Stephen von Haschenperg it was developed into a complicated structure with the tower surrounded by an outer enclosure or 'chemise' which had rounded bastions or 'roundels' projecting from each of its cardinal points. Later a fifth rounded projection was added which contained an entrance porch.

Sandgate fort, much of which has been demolished, was also unusual. Its central keep, which was later converted into a Martello tower, stood within a ward shaped like a triangle with rounded corners which contained three small towers linked by stretches of chemise wall. It was entered via a D-shaped gatetower and a stairway which linked the keep and the outer wall. The lower gun emplacements seem to have been positioned at the curving angles between the towers of the inner chemise and the outer wall.

The fort at Walmer had a circular central tower which was two storeys tall and surrounded by a curtain of a 'quatrefoil' or four-lobed shape that was one storey high. The projecting bastions were so large that there were only very short linking sections of curtain between them. The whole building was surrounded by a wide and deep moat which was crossed by a drawbridge and which would have acted as a killing ground for attackers engaged in a close assault on the fort. Sandown fort, which was lost to the sea, appears to have been similar.

Deal fort was the 'great castle' of the system guarding the Downs and was much larger than the forts at Walmer and Sandown. The central round tower is surrounded by six half-round bastions to produce a 'sexfoil' plan. The tower is three storeys tall and the bastions rise to a height of two storeys, the upper storey and the gun platforms upon the bastions being reached by a spiral staircase running up the centre of the tower. It was surrounded by a moat and numerous low-level gunports for light artillery and muskets allowed a murderous cross fire to be ranged at any force attempting to cross the moat. At St Mawes the central tower was surrounded by three lobes to create a clover-leaf shaped plan. These lobes were partly open but gun positions were provided on their battlements. Facing St Mawes fort across the entrance to Carrick Roads was the Pendennis fort, with a circular gun emplacement concentric to the central tower.

The invasion which Henry VIII expected, and against which he made such expensive provision, never materialised. However, Henry had anticipated the direction of future military development, and as the sense of English nationhood evolved and intensified it was considered increasingly vital that the nation – rather than just the monarchy – should be protected against the consequences of assault from abroad. By the time of Shakespeare Britain was perceived as inhabiting an island set in a silver sea which provided protection against infection and the hand of war. Thereafter any invasion scare, real or imagined, was sure to catalyse a wave of fortification. It is exemplified by Henry's Southsea fort, which was captured in a surprise night attack during the Civil War in 1642 but then strengthened in 1814 during fears of a Napoleonic invasion, improved again in 1850 when an invasion by the forces of Napoleon III was feared, and re-employed during both World Wars.

Serious invasion threats returned in the reign of Henry's daughter, Elizabeth I, and they culminated in the abortive invasion by the Spanish Armada in 1588. The kingdom was still far from secure and in 1545 the French had sent a fleet of 225 ships into the Solent and had sacked the Isle of Wight. In 1548–54 a coastal fort was built at

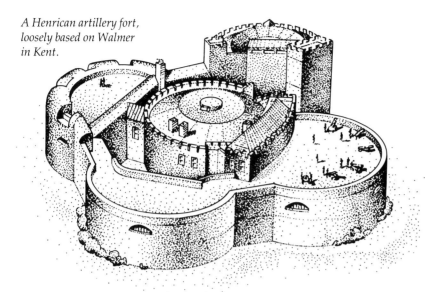

A Henrican artillery fort, loosely based on Walmer in Kent.

Tresco in the Scilly Isles and in 1559–67 another was built at Upnor in Kent to guard warships in the Medway. The queens Mary and Elizabeth both regarded Berwick-on-Tweed as a key position on the northern frontier of the realm and from 1558, at the end of the reign of Mary I (1553–58), the town was fortified according to the latest military standards. Around the perimeter Italian style bastions shaped like arrowheads were built. These projecting gun positions allowed forward and flanking fire and made it possible for the guns on one bastion to protect the artillery positions on its neighbours. The Italian style had developed in Central Italy at the start of the sixteenth century and became widely adopted by the 1540s. Built of earth, these bastions were able to absorb and smother the impact of gunshot and they are well exemplified in the earth-filled defences of Berwick and at Carisbrooke on the Isle of Wight.

Queen Mary entrusted the design of the Berwick defences to Sir Richard Lee. He had begun his career as a military engineer at Calais in the 1530s, designed the fort at Upnor and was regarded as a leading expert on defence. Although not completed to Sir Richard's plans, the fortifications at Berwick are 12 feet (3.6m) thick at the base and 10 feet (3m) thick at the top and faced with smooth-faced masonry. At three corners and midway in the northern curtain are arrowhead bastions or 'mounts'. In the narrow necks of the arrowheads are recesses or 'flankers' defended by

screen walls pierced with gunloops; the flankers were reached from the town by passages through the walls, and from positions on the flankers the walls between the bastions could be swept with fire.

The artillery fort at Deal.

Less sophisticated was the early warning system introduced in 1585 along the invasion coast. Beacons, consisting of iron baskets on long poles which were sited in prominent positions, were intended to be ignited to provide advance warning of an approaching invasion fleet. Some form of beacon system seems to have been used in the twelfth century and in the fourteenth and fifteenth centuries beacons along the south coast were used to warn of French raids. The beacons were lit to warn of the approach of the Spanish Armada and continued to be used until the nineteenth century. In 1804 an accidental firing of Hume Castle beacon near Berwick resulted in the muster of auxiliaries across the Scottish Lowlands.

In the reign of Charles II (1649–85) a fear of Dutch naval power produced new fortifications. Rivalry over the East Indian trade in 1665 resulted in two naval battles between the Dutch and British fleets and in 1667 a Dutch fleet sailed up the Medway, burned sixteen ships and laid waste to Chatham dockyard. Some resistance was offered by a battery which had been hastily installed in the Elizabethan fort at Upnor. The Dutch raid catalysed a new wave of building anti-invasion defences. It was realised that the navy constituted the best guarantee against a successful foreign landing and the work focused on protecting naval bases. A Dutch-born engineer, Sir Bernard de Gomme, was employed to design and execute a series of coastal defence projects according to the latest Continental designs. At first he refortified the Medway and then, between 1670 and 1680, he built the great citadel at Plymouth and designed a new system of fortification for the Tilbury fort. Tilbury was designed to a pentagonal plan with arrowhead bastions at the five corners. The fort was surrounded by a moat and within the moat and opposite the entrance to the fort was a triangular island or 'ravelin' which served as a strongpoint to guard the gates and to cover the northern approaches. Barracks, quarters for officers, storehouses and magazines were housed within the fort, which embodied the latest concepts in military engineering and virtually replaced the earlier fort on the site.

The union of the crowns in 1603 might have brought peace to the northern frontiers of England. However, in 1652 Cromwell sent an army into Scotland and a number of bastion forts were constructed, the most important being at Inverness and Inverlochy. The Inverness fort was abandoned in 1660, but late in the century the Inverlochy fort was reconstructed and renamed 'Fort William' in honour of William of Orange, who became William III in 1689. After the Scottish uprising of 1715 was quashed the government ordered the construction of infantry barracks at strategic places in the Scottish Highlands. Surviving examples include Ruthven Barracks near Kingussie, and Bernera Barracks at Glenelg. They were designed as square courtyards flanked on two sides by massive barrack blocks, while two opposed corners of the perimeter carried projecting rectangular towers which could sweep the approaches with fire, all external walls being pierced with gunloops. A new fort was built at the head of Loch Ness to control movement along the Great Glen in 1729 and work on Fort Augustus continued until 1742. It was attacked by a Jacobite army in 1746 and received a direct hit on the magazine but was rebuilt and garrisoned until 1876. Fort George, on the tip of the Ardersier Peninsula near Inverness, was also slighted by the Jacobite army in 1746 but was then rebuilt as an impregnable artillery fort, part of the chain of British forts which cut the Highlands in half. Work began in 1748 and continued until 1770. A massive curtain wall followed the tapering form of the natural headland and enclosed a defended area of 16 acres (6.5ha). Great projecting angle bastions were provided and on the landward side ditches, bastions and a ravelin made the approaches impregnable. Within these secure defences a garrison of 2000 men was supported.

The building of military roads played an equally important part in the pacification of the Scottish Highlands, allowing troops to be moved swiftly to any trouble spots. Road building began in 1725 to coincide with a new Disarming Act which compelled the clansmen to surrender their weapons. During the decade which followed about 250 miles (400km) of road were completed. During the 1740s the system was extended and work continued into the last third of the century. Much of the road building was supervised by General George Wade, who was appointed as British commander-in-chief in the Highlands in 1724.

In 1803 it was feared that Napoleon was assembling an invasion fleet at Boulogne. The Dungeness-Romney Marsh area was deemed to be vulnerable to invasion and the Royal Military Canal was dug for a distance of 23 miles (37km) from Hythe to Rye to detach the exposed region and to provide a viable defensive line. The canal was 60 feet (18m) wide and 9 feet (2.7m) deep and some 180 guns were allocated to the defences. By the time that it was complete, in 1809, the invasion fears were past. Meanwhile, in 1806 the British authorities had been greatly impressed by the resistance offered to invading British troops by the defenders of a tower at Cap Mortella, in Corsica. It was decided to build a series of similar towers along the southern and eastern shores of England. Cap Mortella tower was 40 feet (12m) tall, 45 feet (13.7m) in diameter and had walls some 13 feet (4m) thick. The ones reproduced in England ranged from 25 feet to 40 feet (7.6 to 12m) tall, were 30 feet to 70 feet (9 to 21m) in diameter and had walls around 8 feet (2.4m) thick. Other examples were built in Canada, the USA and South

Africa and a grand total of almost 150 of these Martello towers were completed, including seventy-four built to guard the low-lying shores of South-Eastern England. Martello towers are two storeys tall with an entrance that is placed about 20 feet (6m) above ground level and reached by a ladder. Inside the towers are vaulted rooms for small garrisons. On their summits are platforms for two or three guns and most Martello towers were moated.

In the middle of the nineteenth century there was a new flurry of invasion scares. It was feared that France, under a new Napoleon, might seek to avenge the French defeat at Waterloo while they also enjoyed a superiority in iron-clad warships mounting highly effective naval guns. A Royal Commission was appointed and recommended the refortification of the Thames, Medway, Milford Haven, Solent and Plymouth areas. Enormous forts were built around Portsmouth and Plymouth according to the fashionable 'polygonal system'. Heavy guns were mounted in shell-proof casements and were intended to prevent invaders reaching any of their main objectives. Each fortress was designed to be self-contained and housed its own barracks.

The 1860 Royal Commission forts represented the last stage in the evolution of the defensive stronghold. During the First World War the bombing of undefended cities by Zeppelins marked the dawn of a new era in warfare, for with the superiority in air power it was possible for any hostile nation to attack the soft inner core of the state directly. As this fact gained recognition warfare became more indiscriminate and more dangerous. Successful defence involved having the right type of defensive armaments in sufficient number. About the time of Hitler's invasion of Austria in the spring of 1938 it appeared that the greatest challenge was posed by Nazi air power and Kingsley Wood, the British air minister, anticipated half-a-million civilian casualties during the first three weeks of an attack. In the middle of the decade experiments were made with Radio Detection (RDF), a primitive form of radar. It was planned to build a chain of twenty RDF stations all along the coast from the Orkneys to the Isle of Wight. At the time in question just five RDF stations were operational, linked by telephone to Fighter Command.

The fighter aircraft available were, however, inadequate and largely outmoded. They numbered about 750, of which only ninety were modern monoplanes, early versions of the Hawker Hurricane. The remainder were biplanes which lacked the speed to overtake some of the German bombers. Only about half of the fighter force was serviceable at any particular time. There was no specialised night fighter force. Anti-aircraft guns were in short supply and scarcely a hundred were available to defend London. Outmoded 3-inch guns were assembled, some, it is alleged, being requisitioned from the Imperial War Museum. Barrage balloons were too few in number to deter low-level bombing.

By the time the threat of invasion had almost become a reality, in 1940, the British defences had expanded to become just adequate. Had the invasion materialised it is debatable whether the destroyers of the Royal Navy would have been able to create havoc among the invasion barges. Had the Germans maintained the Luftwaffe assaults on the fighter airfields rather than switching to the bombing of London or had the attacks on the RDF stations been more determined then the course of history could have been greatly changed. Today there are no strongholds and each citizen, whether young, old or unwilling is a potential combatant in wars which no sane person would wish to fight.

Chapter Nineteen

Corfe Castle, severely
slighted during the Civil
War.

THE DEATH OF CASTLES

In England, as we have seen, the building of castles – as opposed to artillery forts – ended before the medieval period had run its course. Here the evolution of the castle proper was suspended with the completion of the castles of chivalry. Most castles languished in neglect. Each one required constant maintenance but repairs were seldom accomplished and walls were pillaged for stone. It was even possible for Elizabethan and Jacobean commentators to regard castles as the embodiment of evil and to cast a superior glance towards the Continent, where the fashion for fortification developed unabated. In about 1540 John Leland wrote a detailed account of his itinerary and the references which he made to castles have been collected and studied by the architectural historian M. W. Thompson. It is clear from Leland's observations that at the close of the Middle Ages scores of castles were neglected or derelict, and abandoned. Of Belvoir Castle in Leicestershire, Leland wrote:

> Hastings carried much of this led to Ashby de la Zouch where he much built. Then fell all the castle to ruin, and the timber of the roofs uncovered rotted away, and the soil between the walls at the last grew full of elders, and no habitation was there till that of late days the Earl of Rutland hath made it fairer than ever it was.

In Wiltshire he saw Devizes Castle, which was:

> . . . now in ruin, and part of the front of the towers of the gate of the keep and the chapel in it were carried full unprofitably to the building of Master Bainton's place at Bromham scant 3 miles off. There remain divers goodly towers yet in the outer wall of the castle, but all going to ruin . . .

The robbing of castles for stone was evident in many places, as at Elmley in Worcestershire:

> There standith now but one tower and that partly broken. As I went by I saw carts carrying stone thence to amend Pershore Bridge about 11 miles off.

In some places the destruction of a castle was almost complete by the close of the Middle Ages, as at Middleton Stoney in Oxfordshire:

> Some pieces of the walls of it yet little appear; but almost the whole site is overgrown with bushes.

He believed that Tintagel Castle, in Cornwall, had once been a marvellously strong and notable fortress but found:

> . . . sheep now feed within the dungeon. The residue of the buildings of the castle be sore weatherbeaten and in ruin . . .

The site of Worksop Castle in Nottinghamshire was hard to trace, and again stone robbers were blamed:

> . . . the stones of the castle were fetched as some say to make the fair lodge in Worksop Park, not yet finished . . . But I am of the opinion that the canons had the ruins of the castle stones to make the closure of their large walls.

In 1539 the Crown surveyors declared that the castles of Conway, Caernarvon and Harlech were incapable of being defended for one hour should the French or Scots choose to invade. Another survey of Harlech Castle in 1564 found that the interior of every tower was in utter ruin, the hall and chapel were unroofed, the drawbridges had been replaced by crude plank-built structures which were greatly decayed and that the buildings in the courtyard were '. . . utterlie in ruyn and prostrate'.

Such problems with major castles were not new. In 1343 William de Emeldon carried out a survey of five Edwardian castles in Wales and found that at Beaumaris, for example, an expenditure of £684 6s 8d (£684.33) was needed to remedy the defects in the walls, houses, towers and other buildings.

The decay of feudalism and the internal pacification of the realm had made the castle redundant and few could imagine conditions which would return the inland castle to a central position on the military stage. Yet these conditions did occur with the outbreak in 1642 of the Civil War between the Royalist and Parliamentarian factions. Neither side had really been able to prepare for the hostilities, and when they erupted there was little choice but to garrison the decrepit or, at best, ill-prepared castles of the realm. Where time permitted an old stronghold might be surrounded by defensive earthworks, as took place at Donnington Castle, in Berkshire, where the castle was enclosed by pentagonal banks and ditches with three arrowhead bastions. These artillery emplacements allowed fire to be directed at the siegeworks of the attackers.

The war ranged neighbour against neighbour, and since those who still lived in castles or had castles in their grounds were usually supporters of the king it was most common for Royalists to be the besieged party. Many castles were badly damaged by artillery fire, but many more were destroyed or 'slighted'. Sometimes slighting was accomplished for revenge, but most frequently it was done to deny a castle to an enemy during continuing hostilities or during some future uprising. It was also cheaper to slight a captured castle than it was to garrison it. Thompson has quoted Sir John Meldrum, a Parliamentary commander who wrote in justification of his actions at Gainsborough in 1644 as follows:

> . . . I have taken to acquaint your Lordships with what, in my apprehension, I conceive may be both dangerous and unprofitable to this state which is to keep up forts and garrisons which may rather ferment than finish a war. France, Italy and the Low Countries have found by experience during these three hundred years what losses are entailed by places being fortified, while the subjects of the Isle of Britain, through absence thereof, have lived in more tranquility. If Gainsborough had not been razed by my order the enemy might have found a nest to have hatched much mischief at this time.

Normally slighting work was undertaken by the County Committees or Deputy Lieutenants acting under the order of a Parliamentary committee. There are records of the slighting of about 150 castles by the Parliamentarians, but still more castles were probably affected. The destruction could be wrought by gunpowder or by undermining the walls, but normally it was done by workmen wielding pickaxes. Although long since overtaken by developments in warfare several of the old castles put up a stout resistance. The mayor of Pembroke, John Poyer, switched allegiance to the Royalist side and in 1648 the castle was besieged by Parliamentarian forces. Cromwell's troops were kept at bay for seven weeks and the siege only succeeded when the garrison's water supply was captured. Then Poyer was shot and the castle was slighted.

The tensions of living during the Civil War can be exemplified by events at Knaresborough. On hearing that Lord Fairfax was about to seize the castle for Cromwell, Sir Henry Slingsby hastily secured it for the king and shortly afterwards a detachment of militia arrived to form a garrison. In June 1644 the king's nephew, Prince Rupert, arrived from Lancashire and moved towards York, which was under siege. His army met the Parliamentarian and Scottish force at Marston Moor and the Royalists were routed. A fortnight later York surrendered, Fairfax began the reduction of Royalist strongholds in the county and Pontefract, Knaresborough, Scarborough and Helmsley were besieged. In the August Fairfax wrote:

> The small forces I have are employed in several places in this county . . . rather to restrain their incursions upon the country than any hopes I have to take them.

In the meantime the members of Knaresborough garrison had been making themselves thoroughly unpopular by pillaging in the locality. Frustrated and angered by the looting of both the Royalist and Parliamentarian forces local people formed an organisation of 'clubmen' armed with cudgels and makeshift weapons to protect their property. At the same time innocent bystanders sought refuge in the castle. One was Lord Morley and Mounteagle who wrote to Lord Fairfax:

> The inveterate malady of the spleen enforced me to come to the Spa for my old remedy. My stay at Knaresborough to that end has been ever since I wrote to your lordship. I intended to have retired myself to my own home, but was prevented by the sudden coming of your forces. Upon their approach I betook myself with others to the castle not knowing what treaty [treatment] the common sort of soldiers might afford me.

We do not know if he received the safe conduct for himself and his four servants which he requested but a dyer called John Warner was later fined £100 for seeking refuge in the castle.

Just before Christmas in 1644 the garrison at Knaresborough surrendered after a siege and some skirmishing outside the walls. In 1646 Parliament ordered the demolition of several inland castles, and included Knaresborough. The townspeople pleaded that the castle had offered them protection but their pleas were ignored and the work of slighting was carried out in 1648, apparently by using gunpowder to blast out the side of the keep and then proceeding with picks, shovels and crowbars. Then the townspeople appeared like vultures and carted off the stone for their own uses while the more valuable materials, like the lead from the roof, were sold off.

The sale of materials from slighted castles could prove a useful source of revenue to counterbalance the costs of demolition. At Wallingford the demolition of the castle, of which only the gatehouse still stands, cost £450 5s 8d (£450.28), while the sale of materials raised £516 17s 11d (£516.89), leaving an encouragingly tidy profit of about £66.

The degree of demolition varied from place to place. The castles which suffered the most severe and thorough slightings included Bolingbroke, Montgomery, Nottingham, Pontefract, Flint and Sherborne. In some cases the entire side of a keep was removed, as at Scarborough and Helmsley, while at other places the slighting was only sufficient to render the old stronghold untenable. In the case of Montgomery Castle a labour force of about 180 men was employed in the destruction and the bill for wages came to more than £600. Not all the castles destroyed had accommodated Royalist garrisons. Nottingham, for example, had always been in Parliamentary hands and the slighting was accomplished to save the cost of garrisoning while denying it to the enemy. Coastal castles fared better than ones which were inland, for they might always be needed to repel invasions by foreign powers or by Royalist forces. The severe slighting of Scarborough Castle was due to the fact that a Royalist garrison had held it against the Parliamentary troops. In the south the Henrican coastal forts and the castles of Arundel, Bodiam and Herstmonceux were preserved. Not all the work of slighting was accomplished by the Parliamentary side; after the Restoration the strongholds of Parliamentary support, Coventry and Gloucester, had sections of their town walls demolished.

One of the most severe episodes of slighting took place at Corfe Castle, on the island of Purbeck, Dorset. The original castle here was built around 1100, close to the site of an earlier stone hall. It had a plain curtain wall of an oval plan which ringed the highest part of a ridge of the Purbeck Hills. Around 1135 a rectangular keep was built against the inner face of the curtain, to produce a castle of a keep and bailey form. During John's reign a second bailey was added to the west. It was of a triangular form, with a large octagonal tower at its western extremity and D-shaped towers in the northern and southern sections of its curtain. In the reign of Henry III a large outer bailey was added to enclose a section of the ridge to the south-east. The work on the outer gate of this bailey was completed in the reign of Edward I.

In 1634 Corfe Castle was purchased by Sir John Bankes, who was then Attorney General and who became Chief Justice of the Common Pleas. Sir John was a Royalist and in 1642 he joined Charles I in York and followed him to Oxford. Meanwhile his wife and family remained in the castle at Corfe. The castle was unmolested until the

early summer of 1643, when it was besieged by a Parliamentary force led by Sir Walter Erle. Lady Bankes armed and defended the castle and recruited a garrison formed of local tenants and gentry. The castle held for thirteen weeks until the siege was raised when a large cavalry force led by the Earl of Caernarvon arrived in the area. Corfe Castle had survived the attack but the little town below had been destroyed, forcing its inhabitants to seek refuge in the castle. A contemporary account tells that:

> But there passed not many days, before 20 seamen (they in the castle not suspecting any such thing) came very early in the morning to demand the pieces [guns]; the lady in person

Ruins of the severely slighted castle at Montgomery.

(early as it was) goes to the gates and desires to see their warrant; they produce one, under the hand of some of the Commissioners; but instead of delivering them, though at the time there were but five men in the castle, yet these five assisted by their maid-servants, at the lady's command mounted these pieces on their carriages again, and loaded one of them they gave fire, which small thunder so affrighted the seamen that they all quitted the castle and ran away. They being gone, by beat of drum she summoned help into the castle and upon the alarm given a very considerable guard of tenants and friends came to her assistance, there being withal some fifty arms brought into the castle from several parts of the island; this guard was kept into the castle about a week. During this time many threatening letters were sent unto the lady telling her what great forces should be sent to fetch them if she would not by fair means be persuaded to deliver them; and to deprive her of her auxiliaries, all or most of them being neighbours thereabouts, they threaten that if they oppose the delivery of them they would fire their houses; presently their wives come to the castle, where they weep and wring their hands, and with clamorous oratory persuade their husbands to come home, and not by saving others to expose their own houses to spoil and ruin. Now to reduce the castle into a distressed condition, they did not only intercept two-hundred weight of powder, provided against a siege, but they interdict them the liberty of common markets. Proclamation is made at Wareham (a market town hard by) that no beef, no beer, or other provisions should be sold to Lady Bankes or for her use; strict watches are kept that no messenger shall pass in or out of the castle . . .

At the start of 1644 the Royalist cause was ascendant but then its fortunes deteriorated. In midsummer Dorset fell to the Parliamentarians and Corfe Castle was again held for the king. Lady Bankes held the castle through the winter and her troubles were magnified when she learned of the death, in Oxford a few days after Christmas, of her husband. On 28 October 1645, it was ordered that the siege of Corfe should be intensified and two regiments were placed at the disposal of the Governor of Poole. Then events took an unlikely course. A troop of 120 Royalists under a man with the inappropriate name of Cromwell left Oxford to relieve the defenders of Corfe and kidnapped the Governor of Wareham and two Commissioners. The hostages were carried through the siege lines and into the castle. However, after Cromwell's troop had left the castle they were captured. Now a hostage in Corfe Castle, the Governor of Wareham sought to subvert the garrison and a hostile force was smuggled into the castle and the keep was seized. Lady Bankes was allowed to leave the castle with her family and dependents, but all her property was forfeited.

Corfe Castle was surrendered on 27 February 1646, and on 5 March the House of Commons voted to have it demolished. Probably because of the remarkable resistance and resolution shown by Lady Bankes the slighting was more severe than was necessary to render the castle unfit for military use. The northern half of the keep was demolished and great gaps were blown in the curtain walls.

Another castle which suffered greatly was Sherborne Old Castle in Dorset. During the Civil War the owner, Lord Digby, was one of the principal advisors to the king. The castle was held for the Royalist cause in 1642 and again in 1645. In 1645 a fullscale siege was mounted by forces under the Parliamentary general Fairfax. Cromwell was at this time his second-in-command, and he regarded Sherborne as 'a malicious and mischievous castle, like its owner'. Under the leadership of Sir Lewis Dyre, Lord Digby's stepson, the castle resisted for sixteen days before being stormed on 15 August. Parliament then ordered the castle to be dismantled and it has existed as a ruin ever since.

The last Royalist castle to surrender to Parliamentary siege was Harlech. On 15 March 1647 the constable, Colonel William Owen of Brogyntyn, released the fourteen gentlemen and twenty-eight common soldiers who were the surviving members of the garrison and this marked the end of the Civil War. Although it was ordered that the castle should be rendered untenable the main structure of Harlech survived slighting intact.

After the Civil War the great majority of castles in England and Wales existed as empty, ruinous places, although in Scotland and Ireland the tower houses often remained in occupation. The redundancy and decay of castles created conditions in which completely unfortified stately homes could multiply, so that while aristocrats on the Continent frequently occupied old castles which were variously enlarged or adapted during the passing years, the English aristocrat was typically found residing in a classical mansion built from scratch in a consistent and fashionable style. When castle life was no more than a distant memory it could be romanticised and the Gothic Revival produced many parodies of the old military architecture. One of the last great country houses to be built was Castle Drogo in Devon, designed by Sir Edwin Lutyens and erected between 1911 and 1930 and recalling the external appearance of a castle of the thirteenth century.

The castle was very much a creature of its times. It echoed the anxieties of its age and embodied defensive features which were direct responses to the latest technologies in offensive warfare. But when moats, battlements and gatehouses became redundant they were still incorporated into aristocratic houses because, after centuries of use, they had become the indispensable symbols of nobility.

GLOSSARY

Adulterine castle A castle not licensed by the monarch.

Bailey A courtyard or ward of the castle defended by a rampart and palisade or curtain wall.

Ballista An early artillery weapon resembling a large crossbow fixed to a movable carriage and firing large arrows or metal bolts.

Balustrade An ornamental parapet.

Barbican An outwork defending the gate of a castle or town, often built as an outer extension of the gate.

Barmkin The defended courtyard of a Scottish castle.

Bartizan An overhanging corner turret.

Bastle A fortified house or farmstead of the Anglo-Scottish borderlands.

Batter The outward sloping masonry at the base of the wall of a castle which was built to resist attempts at undermining.

Bawn The defended courtyard of an Irish tower house.

Belfry A mobile timber tower employed in siege warfare which could be rolled up to the castle walls. When the drawbridge at the top of the belfry was lowered, attackers could emerge and attempt to storm the battlements.

Berm A level area between the outer foot of the castle walls and the moat.

Bivallate fort A hillfort with two sets of ramparts and ditches. A multivallate fort has more than two sets and a univallate fort has only one.

Bratticing, bratishing A timber gallery built on beams projecting in front of the battlements allowing missiles or burning pitch to be dropped on to attackers at the base of the walls.

Bore, pick A battering ram which was tipped in iron and used for attacking the masonry at the base of a wall.

Brochs Small fortresses occupied by the Scottish aristocracy between the first and third centuries BC.

Bronze Age c. 2500–650 BC.

Burh Saxon fortified settlements.

Castellation Decorative battlements.

Chevaux-de-frise Jagged stones set upright to guard the approaches to a stronghold.

Constable, castellan The governor of a castle.

Corbel Projecting stonework used to support an overhanging parapet.

Counterscarp A bank on the outer face of a ditch.

Crannogs Artificial islands of brushwood, stakes and rubble built in lakes to carry dwellings.

Crenellation A crenel was the gap or 'embrasure' in the battlements. A licence to crenellate was a royal permit to build fortifications.

Curtain A lofty wall enclosing a bailey or courtyard.

Dark Ages AD 410–AD 1066.

Donjon A keep or great tower.

Embrasure *See* Crenellation.

Forebuilding A foreward defensive building screening the entrance of a keep or castle from direct attack.

Freestone A stone which can be sawn into smooth-faced blocks.

Garderobe A lavatory.

Glacis The slope from the outer edge of a ditch to level ground.

Hall The principal public room in a medieval castle.

Hoarding *See* Bratticing.

Iron Age 650 BC–AD 43.

Juliet A small round tower.

Keep The great tower of an eleventh-century or twelfth-century castle.

Machicolation Openings in the floor of a projecting platform or parapet through which missiles and other unwelcome materials could be dropped on to attackers below.

Mangonel A siege engine which launched heavy stones.

Mantlet A screening wall built in front of another wall.

Merlons The high sections of a parapet which separate the crenels.

Meurtrieres Small openings above and just inside a door through which missiles could be thrust at an attacker.

Motte A castle mound of the Norman period.

Murder holes *See* Meurtrieres.

Neolithic Age 5000–2500 BC.

Oppida Pre-Roman native capitals, generally fortified with earthen outworks.

Palisade A protective wall built of closely spaced upright stakes.

Parapet The wall protecting the outer side of a wall walk.

Pavise A movable protective screen.

Pele Defensive tower of the Anglo-Scottish borderlands.

Pit prison A prison cell entered only through a hatch in the ceiling.

Portcullis A strong timber or iron grill which could be lowered by winches in the gatehouse to protect a gate.

Postern A small gate, sometimes concealed, which served as a minor entrance to a castle and through which defenders might slip to launch a surprise attack.

Quarrel A missile fired from a crossbow.

Quatrefoil Shaped like a four-leaved clover.

Rath An ancient farmstead surrounded by one or more circular earthbanks.

Ravelin A detached outwork protecting the salient of a bastion.

Reentrant The inner angle in a wall.

Revetment Reinforcements built to protect the face of an earthbank.

Roman Age AD 43–AD 410.

Sallyport *See* Postern.

Sarsen stone A hard stone which once formed a capping on the Marlborough Downs (fragments were incorporated into the stone circles of Stonehenge and Avebury).

Sexfoil A shape with six lobes.

Solar The private living chamber of a lord.

Ward *See* Bailey.

Yett Iron portcullis employed in some Scottish castles.

SOME IDEAS FOR FURTHER READING

Braun, H., *The English Castle*, Batsford, 1936.

Brown, R. Allen, *English Castles*, Chancellor Press, 1970 edn.

Burke, John, *Life in the Castle in Medieval England*, Batsford, 1978.

Cathcart King, D. J., *The Castle in England and Wales*, Croom Helm, 1988.

Dyer, James, *Hillforts of England and Wales*, Shire, 1981.

Forde-Johnston, James, *A Guide to the Castles of England and Wales*, Constable, 1981.

Fry, P.S., *Medieval Castles*, David and Charles, 1975.

Guilbert, Graeme, *Hill-Fort Studies, For A. H. A. Hogg*, Leicester University Press, 1981.

Hogg, A. H. A., *Hill-Forts of Britain*, Hart-Davis MacGibbon, 1975.

Gies, J. and F., *Life in a Medieval Castle*, Aberlard-Schuman, 1975.

Morley, B. M., *Henry VIII and the Development of Coastal Defence*, HMSO, 1976.

Illingworth, J. L., *Yorkshire's Ruined Castles*, S. R. Publishers, 1970.

Long, Brian, *Castles of Northumberland*, Harold Hill, 1967.

O'Neil, B. H. St J., *Castles, An Introduction to the Castles of England and Wales*, HMSO, 1973.

Platt, Colin, *The Castle in Medieval England and Wales*, Secker and Warburg, 1982.

Reid, Alan, *The Castles of Wales*, George Philip, 1973.

Simpson, W. Douglas, *Exploring Castles*, Routledge and Kegan Paul, 1957.

Steane, John M., *The Archaeology of Medieval England and Wales*, Croom Helm, 1985.

Thompson, M. W., *The Decline of the Castle*, Cambridge University Press, 1987.

Toy, Sidney, *The Castles of Great Britain*, Heinemann, 1953.
Castles, Their Construction and History, Dover Publications, 1985.

CASTLES AND STRONGHOLDS WITH SUBSTANTIAL REMAINS – GAZETTEER

ENGLAND

Avon
Thornbury

Berkshire
Donnington Castle
Windsor Castle

Buckinghamshire
Boarstall (NT)

Cambridgeshire
Longthorpe Tower

Cheshire
Beeston
Chester

Cornwall
Cotehele
Launceston
Restormel Castle
St Mawes
Tintagel Castle

Cumbria
Appleby
Brough Castle
Carlisle
Sizergh Castle (NT)

Derbyshire
Bolsover
Peveril Castle

Devon
Castle Drogo (NT)
Dartmouth Castle
Exeter
Lydford
Totnes

Dorset
Corfe Castle (NT)
Sandsfoot
Sherborne Old Castle

Durham
Durham
Lumley

East Sussex
Bodiam Castle (NT)
Camber
Hastings
Herstmonceux Castle
Pevensey
Rye

Essex
Colchester Castle
Hedingham Castle
Layer Marney Towers

Gloucestershire
Sudeley Castle

Hampshire
Portchester

Hereford and Worcester
Goodrich Castle
Kilpeck
Longtown Castle
Richards Castle

Hertfordshire
Berkhamsted

Humberside
Wressle

Isle of Wight
Carisbrooke

Kent
Deal
Dover
Hever Castle
Lympne
Rochester Castle
Sandown
Tonbridge

Upnor
Walmer

Lancashire
Lancaster

Leicestershire
Ashby de la Zouch Castle
Kirby Muxloe Castle
Leicester

Lincolnshire
Lincoln
Tattershall Castle

Norfolk
Baconsthorpe Castle
Caister Castle
Castle Acre
Castle Rising
New Buckenham
Norwich
Oxburgh Hall (NT)
Thetford

Northumberland
Alnwick
Aydon Castle
Bamburgh
Berwick-on-Tweed
Dunstanburgh Castle (NT)
Norham Castle
Warkworth Castle

North Yorkshire
Bolton Castle
Helmsley Castle
Knaresborough Castle
Markenfield Hall
Middleham Castle
Nappa Hall
Pickering
Richmond
Scarborough
Sherriff Hutton Castle

Skipton Castle
York

Oxfordshire
Greys Court (NT)
Oxford

Shropshire
Clun Castle
Ludlow
Redcastle
Stokesay Castle

Somerset
Nunney Castle

South Yorkshire
Conisbrough
Tickhill

Staffordshire
Tamworth

Suffolk
Framlingham
Orford
Mettingham Castle

Surrey
Abinger Motte
Farnham Castle

Tyne and Wear
Newcastle

Warwickshire
Compton Wynyates
Kenilworth
Maxstoke
Warwick Castle

West Midlands
Dudley

West Sussex
Arundel

West Yorkshire
Pontefract

Wiltshire
Ludgershall

SCOTLAND

Central
Doune Castle
Stirling Castle

Dumfries and Galloway
Threave Castle

Grampian
Castle Fraser
Craigievar
Kildrummy

Highland
Fort Augustus
Fort George
Fort William

Lothian
Edinburgh Castle

Strathclyde
Rothesay Castle

Tayside
Claypotts Castle

WALES

Clwyd
Caergwrle
Chirk (NT)
Denbigh
Flint
Hawarden Castle
Rhuddlan

Dyfed
Aberystwyth
Carew
Cilgerran (NT)
Kidwelly

Llanstephan
Llawhaden
Manorbier Castle
Pembroke
Tenby

Gwent
Caldicote Castle
Chepstow
Grosmont Castle
Monmouth
Raglan Castle
Skenfrith Castle (NT)
White Castle

Gwynedd
Beaumaris
Caernarvon
Castell-y-Bere
Harlech
Conway Castle
Criccieth
Degannwy
Dolbardarn Castle
Dolwyddelan Castle

Powys
Aberedw Castle
Cefnllys
Montgomery Castle
Tretower

Glamorgan
Caerphilly
Cardiff
Castell Coch
Weobley Castle

REPUBLIC OF IRELAND

Co. Clare
Bunratty Castle

County Meath
Trim Castle

INDEX